T0198862

Messages FROM Assisi

The Life and Teachings of
St. Francis of Assisi for Today

Father Kevin J. Haines

authorHOUSE®

AuthorHouse™
1663 Liberty Drive
Bloomington, IN 47403
www.authorhouse.com
Phone: 1 (800) 839-8640

© *2018 Father Kevin J. Haines. All rights reserved.*

No part of this book may be reproduced, stored in a retrieval system, or
transmitted by any means without the written permission of the author.

Published by AuthorHouse 07/30/2018

ISBN: 978-1-5462-4094-5 (sc)
ISBN: 978-1-5462-4093-8 (e)

Library of Congress Control Number: 2018905371

Print information available on the last page.

Any people depicted in stock imagery provided by Getty Images are models,
and such images are being used for illustrative purposes only.
Certain stock imagery © Getty Images.

This book is printed on acid-free paper.

Because of the dynamic nature of the Internet, any web addresses or links contained in
this book may have changed since publication and may no longer be valid. The views
expressed in this work are solely those of the author and do not necessarily reflect the
views of the publisher, and the publisher hereby disclaims any responsibility for them.

Scripture quotations marked NASB are taken from the New American
Standard Bible®, Copyright © 1960, 1962, 1963, 1968, 1971, 1972, 1973,
1975, 1977, 1995 by The Lockman Foundation. Used by permission.

Contents

Introduction

I confess to you upfront that I love being a parish priest! I know it is not for everyone, but it was God's will for me. One of the many things that they don't tell you before you are ordained is how much love, peace, and sense of belonging that you are going to experience. It has been my greatest honor to serve God and His people in this way. My name is Father Kevin J. Haines. I am a diocesan priest of the Diocese of Lafayette-in-Indiana. I have been a priest for just over twenty-three years now. I am currently assigned to St. Maria Goretti Parish in Westfield, Indiana (a suburb just north of Indianapolis). In the late summer and early fall of 2010, I journeyed to Assisi, Italy to spend time with God, to learn more about His servant and Saint, Francis of Assisi, and to discover what both God and St. Francis would have to say to me, possibly other priests, Catholics, other Christians, and even non-believers in this day and age. The words on these pages that follow are my attempt to allow you to journey with me at this time in my life, allowing St. Francis of Assisi to lead all of us closer to God, especially to His Son, Jesus Christ, and to each other in the Church.

I have been very blessed to have this sabbatical time from duties as a parish priest through the generosity of the Eli Lilly Foundation and their Clergy Renewal Grant program for those who minister in Indiana. Two years ago, in 2008, a committee from St. Maria Goretti approached me about applying for one of these grants. I allowed them to, having no idea how much effort and work they would end up putting into it. In June of 2009, we received word that I had in fact received a grant and preparations were made for my journey to Assisi. I thank the Eli Lilly Foundation. I thank our parish family and most especially the committee who made this possible. And I thank my diocese for encouraging me and supporting me in this endeavor.

I have always had a certain affinity for St. Francis of Assisi. I remember as a small child even, being fascinated by the statues, and holy cards, and other pictures of the young saint in the brown robe with the funny haircut. I loved the stories of him giving all his possessions away, and the Crucifix speaking to him, and when he preached to the birds or spoke to the wolf, or when praying he received the Stigmata, the wounds of Christ in his own flesh. As a child, as a youth, and even as a young man there was always something captivating about this Saint! I have always found St. Francis of Assisi to be one of those saints that you just always wanted to know more about! Perhaps if you picked up this book or downloaded it, you maybe feel the same way. St. Francis of Assisi is fascinating. He draws us in to his story.

I first came to Assisi back in 1983, when I was a first-year graduate student at the North American College in Rome, beginning my theological studies. I came with my classmates. It was part of North American's ritual of welcome for its new students, or as they call them "new men". Assisi is much more than another quaint little Italian village. There is a certain spirit there. I fell in love with it immediately.

It is also worth saying that while I have the greatest respect for those who answered the call to Franciscan life in their vocation, and after a good deal of prayer and discernment, I knew for sure that I was not called to be a Franciscan. I was extremely attracted for a couple of years to the life of a Missionary of Charity, St. Teresa of Calcutta's order for both women and men. I, like many in the Catholic Church, consider the Missionaries of Charity to be the newest interpretation of what St. Francis of Assisi was trying to accomplish back in the thirteenth century. Ultimately, that was not where God was calling me either. I have many parishioners who are grateful for that. But that doesn't mean that "the rest of us" don't have much to learn from this holy saint.

In fact, I'd like to suggest that the world and the Church today need the example, the experience, and the teaching of St. Francis of Assisi now more than ever. We live in a world that has, in many ways, abandoned God. We move ourselves farther and farther away from His Holy Presence and His Holy Will, and then we scratch our heads and wonder where God is. Many are completely lost in the world today. Read any paper. Watch any newscast. Visit the popular websites. The evidence is there every day! God has become less and less relevant to so many. His Son, Jesus Christ, was supposed to be the solution to that problem. Jesus is the connection between God and man. His Mother, Mary, also was supposed to help all of us by being the mediatrix for us. And yet for so many, and I see this every day as a parish priest, both Jesus and Mary are so far away from our own experiences. They are too perfect. One was, we believe, Divine and the other was, again we believe, Immaculate. It is hard to get beyond that when you are struggling every day just to keep trying not to give up on being better in the middle of a world that in many ways already has. We need someone more like us to be our example. Enter Francis. Francis was from a world of wealth and privilege. He had everything that today we are told we are to want in this life. He had it all! He was young and charismatic and popular. He liked beautiful maidens, fast horses, and the next good time. Poverty, the trials of life, sickness, and even death were not concerns of Francis as a young man. Sound familiar? How many of us live that same way? We, like Francis, also go through the motions of practicing our faith. Maybe we go to Mass and maybe we don't. Maybe we go to Confession, and even more likely, maybe we don't. Maybe we pray daily and think about God in our lives, and maybe we don't, or at least we don't often enough. In early twenty-first century America, we are a lot more like Francis before his conversion than we'd like to admit. And that's why his story, applied to our lives, is so very important for us as Catholic Christians today! Or for any of us who dare to call ourselves a "Christian" today.

It was Mahatma Gandhi who wrote back in the 1940's that he didn't have any problem with Jesus or with Christianity in general. Gandhi's biggest problem with Christianity and with the Church was that no one ever really lived the Christian faith. The one exception to that biting statement, according to Gandhi, was St. Francis of Assisi. According to this non-Christian, the closest that we have come to living like Christ is St. Francis of Assisi. Here's a lesson for us all. Let us pay attention. Let us learn from "the little poor man" of Assisi.

The great peace and sense of tranquility that oozes from the walls and streets and churches of Assisi, remind us that something very special happened here back in the thirteenth century. The Catholic Church was changed forever by a movement that began within these walls and on the side of this mountain. God began that movement with a young man named Francis, who we are going to be talking a lot about in the following pages. But what is also true is that the movement began to spread immediately to other young people in this small town. Something very strange and wonderful and powerful was happening to the affluent, upwardly-mobile, young people of Assisi. It must have seemed unbelievable to their families and friends. God was changing their lives in a very powerful way. Eventually, through St. Francis and later St Clare, and all of the early followers, God would change many other lives down through the ages and around the world, young and old, rich and poor.

As you spend this time with these words on the following pages, dear reader, the only other real question is, are YOU willing to let God change you through the story of St. Francis of Assisi? Or is this just another book of words for you to add to your library?

I thank all of those down through the years who gave me the gift of faith, and who like St. Francis, showed me Jesus. There are simply too many of you to start naming people, but know that I treasure each and every one of you. I do want to thank the wonderful Janet Thompson and awesome Deb Krupowicz for all their help in the final editing of this book. I especially thank my parents, Ken and Rosann Haines, who first evangelized the faith to me. Dad, thank you and I love you. I dedicate this book to the memory of my mother, Rosann, who died from pancreatic cancer a month before I was to leave for Assisi to begin writing this book. Mom, I love you and miss you. And I know how pleased you would be! And hey, in Heaven, look up the little man from Assisi, I think that the two of you will have much to talk about.

In Christ Jesus,

Fr. Kevin J. Haines
Assisi, Italy
2010

"MESSAGES FROM ASSISI" - DISCUSSION GUIDELINE QUESTIONS

The Introduction

A. What attracts YOU to St. Francis? Why are you here today? What do you want Franciscan spirituality to do for you in your life?

B. As we start today, what do you see as St. Francis' greatest message to our world today? What would he say to the Church of today? What would he like and what would he dislike?

C. How can this little Saint from Assisi help all of us to better today? What would we have to do to have the same kind of peace that St. Francis had nearly 800 years ago? Would you have considered joining St. Francis or St. Clare if you were alive 800 years ago?

CHAPTER ONE

The Joy Of St. Francis Of Assisi - Part I

"Where there is poverty and joy, there is neither covetousness nor avarice."

(St. Francis of Assisi)

Any discussion, class, book, blog, or conversation about St. Francis of Assisi, *il Poverello*, has to begin with his great joy. St. Francis was charismatic! Even before his conversion, as young man, St. Francis was bringing people together. There is even evidence of this when he was small child. He was fun; he was exuberant. He was the life the party! Many believe that his charisma certainly must have disappeared on the way to sainthood. Saints aren't fun. (Just read the life of St. Jerome sometime!) Yet, as we begin our story, we have to recognize that St. Francis didn't lose his joy, his enthusiasm, or his charisma after his conversion. Instead, St. Francis's joy was made more complete. It was given a stronger foundation. If before his conversion, Frances di Bernardone was the "life of the party", the instigator of joy-filled activities and adventures, the one who gathered people together, this happened only more so when St. Francis's life was centered not on the frivolity of the world, but on God's everlasting kingdom!

In his conversion, St. Francis found new meaning for his joy. His happiness wasn't based on the next party or celebration with his friends, or on his next bigger, faster horse, or on his success as a knight. St. Francis found much greater joy in his experience of the love of Christ. Christ and Francis's newly discovered holiness became his new goal of life and a new source of joy and happiness. Following his conversion, St. Francis drank in his new-found Christian spirituality with the same fervor that he used to drink wine with his friends.

St. Francis's new joy would become one of the principle hallmarks of his life, his community, and his spirituality. This particular saint that we seek to understand and emulate in our lives was a genuinely joy-filled person. Even dirt poor, having given away everything that he had, and roaming the Umbrian countryside begging for food and shelter and asking for money to re-build local churches, St. Francis of Assisi didn't act like a beggar, or a poor man, or a man who had the weight of the Church on his shoulders. St. Francis was happy; he was always singing. He had a smile on his face. He was truly filled with the peace that comes only from knowing that one is truly doing the Holy Will of God!

This is so important for us to understand today. God offers all of us that same peace, and joy, and happiness. And He offers it not in some passing, you're-going-to-be-happy-for-a-couple-of-days sort of way. He is offering it to us forever. And that ought to give us even more joy!

St. Francis had profound joy whether he was preaching to the birds or converting unbelievers. Doing God's work electrified this saint! His enthusiasm was contagious! His first followers were drawn to join him within weeks of his starting his new life. It didn't take years or even months. Did the affluent young men of Assisi really see themselves joining up with their old pal and living as beggars for the rest of their lives? Francis's own father, some members of his own family, and many of the townsfolk of Assisi considered young Francis crazy. Why weren't those first followers of St. Francis more concerned about their being linked to a lunatic? Is sanctity really that attractive? Today we presume not. They don't make movies or write book or sing songs any more about the holy. We presume that holiness is linked to dullness and boredom and tediousness. And that's a shame. We have profaned the Holy and so watered-down our experience of God, that we go through the motions of what we are supposed to be doing. Shame on us as Church for so perverting the Gospel message! We would do well to re-think our culture's misconceptions, and there is no one better to help us change our minds than St. Francis of Assisi.

St. Francis would tell us that we, as Christians, and most especially as Catholic Christians, have more to be joy-filled about than anyone else. We too have been called and chosen by God. We all need to know that. We are given our lives to praise and glorify Him and to love and serve Him in His Holy Church. It is exciting work! It is challenging work. It is not all going to be sitting around a campfire singing "Kumbaya" and roasting marshmallows, but there are going to be times of extraordinary joy as we serve God and watch Him work through us right in front of our eyes. We too are to be instruments of God. Think about that for just a second. All of us are called! St. Francis wanted nothing more than for everyone to find his or her place in God's Kingdom, whether as a brother, or a sister, or mother, or a father, or as a priest, or as a single person. Everybody has been offered unexplainable joy and peace.

Where is that joy and peace in us? Sometimes I look at good Christian people who just don't look like people who have been redeemed by our Lord, Jesus Christ. Look around you at Mass next Sunday. Would you want to be part of your community, judging by the joy and peace that is evident on the people's faces around you? And I'm not talking about some giddy, hokey, fake joy or pretend enthusiasm, like on some religious shows on TV. I'm talking about the real thing. I'm talking about the kind of enthusiasm that makes you want to join up and get involved and help out and dedicate your life to something much, much bigger than all of us. That's the kind of joy that we need in the Church today. And that's the kind of joy that St. Francis of Assisi had in every thing that he did.

I start with this because this is why we need this saint. The joy and enthusiasm of St. Francis is exactly what we need in the Church today to continue the re-building process that St. Francis was commanded to begin back in the thirteenth century. The Gospel and the Church will never be relevant in the world today until we start giving an attractive and deeper alternative to the life that this world and the devil offer and make look so attractive. We have something much better. Isn't it time we let it show? Isn't it time that we let people know about it? Isn't it time again for people to look at us as Church and say, "Hey, I want to be part of that!"?

The essence of joy that is truly fruit of the Holy Spirit has been promised to us by Christ Himself. We are never going to discover that true joy if we continually fill our hearts and souls with temporary, fake joy. St. Francis knew this. It is why he had to get away from all attractions, and all distractions. The joys of the world will never fulfill us because they never last. Those people in the commercials all look so happy in their new car or using their new computer or wearing their new clothes. But what's the reality? We get the new car or the new computer or the new clothes, and maybe we're happy for a brief while. Eventually we've got to come up with the next "thing" that is going to make us happy, and we hope and pray that somehow that happiness will last longer next time, but it never does. It's a game. It's a game that St. Francis and the early Franciscans refused to play. And remember, the first Franciscans and Poor Clares were young people who could afford a lot of "things". They knew that there had to be more. They found it in Christ through the example of St Francis.

Do we know that there's got to be more? Are we seeking authentic joy in our lives?

"Come to me, all of you who labor and are burdened, and I will give you rest. Take my yoke upon you and learn from me, for I am meek and humble of heart; and you will find rest for yourselves. For my yoke is easy, and my burden light."

Gospel of St. Matthew 11:28-30

"MESSAGES FROM ASSISI" - DISCUSSION GUIDELINE QUESTIONS

Chapter #1 - The Joy of St. Francis of Assisi - Part I -

A. Can you think of an example in your life of your Faith experience that gave you great joy? Is it reasonable to expect God to give us that mountain-top experience of joy all the time? What did St. Francis do when he didn't "feel" particularly joyful?

B. What would it take for us to make our communities more joyful? What the greatest challenge facing our communities when it comes to our joy? What would it take for us to make our Catholic Christian communities more attractive to outsiders?

C. How do we get the message out that there's more to life than our things? How does the Church have any chance of competing with TV or the movies or the internet? What aren't we emphasizing about our Faith that we should be, to make it more real and more important to others?

CHAPTER TWO

Humility

"Where there is patience and humility, there is neither anger nor worry."

St. Francis of Assisi

I n the first weeks and months following his conversion, humility must have been easier for St. Francis of Assisi. After all, he had taken off his clothes and given them back to his father in the heart of downtown Assisi. He had left his family, his friends, his old life, and even his affluence all behind. One would imagine that it would be easy to be humble when you own nothing and are living on Divine Providence every day. Many people already had a low opinion of young Francis. Many thought him crazy or mentally ill. In those days it must have been easier for the saint to be completely humble before God and others. But things did not stay that way. Very soon others came to join St. Francis. They would look to him for spiritual leadership and guidance.

As their reputation for genuine holiness and for their extraordinary work for God with the poor and the sick and with churches that had fallen into disrepair began to grow, staying humble would become one of the greatest struggles for St. Francis and his companions. St. Francis and his early followers knew all too well that pride and the glorification of self were the devil's favorite tools. It is somewhat easy to understand, then, why humility also became such an important mark of Franciscan spirituality. If our Lord and Savior Jesus Christ is truly to be our all and all, then we must get out of the way completely. St. Francis knew this before he started his order. How much more important it became later after his order met with early success. For St. Francis, it was absolutely imperative to stay as humble as possible, always giving the glory and praise to God Who truly was and is the Source of all goodness.

There is a wonderful story from the *Actus* about St. Francis and Brother Masseo of Marignano concerning humility. Brother Masseo was a man of great holiness in his own right. He was a frequent companion of St. Francis in the early days of the order. Br. Masseo asked St. Francis one day, straight out, "Why after you? Why after you? Why after you?" Brother Masseo asked this to test the saint. He explained that the whole world wanted to see Francis, and hear him, and obey him. He reminded the saint that he was not strong, or powerful, or rich, or extremely wise or learned, or even attractive in the eyes of the world. Why him? St. Francis lowered his head in prayer and rejoiced greatly in his soul. After a few moments, he came back to himself and answered Brother Masseo. "You really want to know why? I have this from the all-holy eyes of God that see the good and evil everywhere. For those blessed and all-holy eyes have not seen among sinners anyone more vile or insufficient than I am. God chose me because He could not find on earth a creature more vile than me, to do that most wonderful work that He intends to do. God has chosen the foolish things of the world to put to shame the wise, and God has chosen the base things of the world and the despised, to bring to naught the noble, the great, and the strong, so that excellence in virtue may truly be from God." St. Francis' answer deeply moved Brother Masseo, as it should all of us.

We must all remember to maintain a perspective of humility when it comes to our dealing with God. "He is God and we are not" is many times the answer to our questions. We, like St. John the Baptist, must become less and less so that He can become more and more. St. Francis lived that out in a powerful way in his own life. He used to shrink from fame and acclamation that became so much a part of his life in the latter years. The brothers would hide him from the throngs of folks who just wanted to see him or hear him or touch him. In spite of our ridiculing sanctity and holiness, even today, nearly eight hundred years later, we too are attracted to genuine holiness. It fascinates us; it calls and beckons us. Even if we know in our hearts how truly far away from that holiness we are, we are still attracted to the holiness of God's special ones because they remind us of what we all can be.

As a young man studying in Rome in the mid-1980's, I was privileged to have several experiences with both Saint John Paul II and Saint Teresa of Calcutta. My most profound memories of each of them are how they electrified huge crowds of people, no matter where they went in the world. Here, two modern saints were granted rock star/ movie star/ sports star status because of their holiness and sanctity! Saint John Paul and Saint Teresa of Calcutta didn't make movies, or write songs, or score winning goals (actually, in the case of Saint John Paul, his poetry has been set to music, but that doesn't necessarily qualify him as a rock star), and yet everywhere that they went, there were those massive crowds of people, many of them young people, who were mesmerized by their faith, holiness, and love. How many times did I see tears of great joy streaming down the faces of young people, simply by being in the presence of such holiness? Certainly St. Francis encountered the same in his travels in the thirteenth century. Mankind is mesmerized by what we can be, if we truly let God be God in our lives.

St. Francis and his friars were always choosing the "little" way. This would have a profound impact later on St. Teresa the Little Flower. Nothing was for their own glory. It was ALL for the glory and praise of God. And when they, and we, let it be that way, miracles happen. We don't do it; God does it through us. St. Francis was keenly aware of his weaknesses, his sinfulness, and his limitations. But that didn't stop him from offering to God everything that he was and everything that he had so that God could use him as He saw fit. And look what happened! He changed the Church, and he changed the world.

Another of my favorite stories from the *Actus* is the story of how St. Francis sent Brother Rufino to preach in Assisi without his habit. I think that this demonstrates very vividly the playfulness that often accompanied St. Francis' lessons on humility. Brother Rufino was a holy friar. He was such a great prayer warrior that he would spend hours in deep contemplation. Because of being so prayerful, Brother Rufino gave up nearly all other talking and speaking. It is said that he had neither the gift nor the ability to preach the Word of God. So one day St. Francis came to him and asked him to go and preach in a church in Assisi. Brother Rufino humbly acknowledged his lack of skill at preaching, and he asked that St. Francis send someone else on this mission. "I am just a simple and ignorant fellow," Brother Rufino offered. St. Francis, in response to his insubordination, told him to go immediately to preach in Assisi and that now he was to go wearing only his undergarments. Brother Rufino without hesitation immediately obeyed, stripped off his habit, and went to preach in Assisi. He entered the church, knelt in reverence before the altar, and then went up to the pulpit and began preaching. The townsfolk laughed at him, wondering aloud if St. Francis and his followers had done so much penance that they had all lost their minds.

Meanwhile, St. Francis began to have second thoughts about the mission on which he had sent Brother Rufino. Before he was a friar, Brother Rufino was one of the foremost gentlemen of Assisi, a noble man. By God's inspiration, St. Francis decided that he should experience himself what he had ordered Br. Rufino to do. St. Francis stripped off his garments and, accompanied by Brother Leo who discretely carried both Francis' and Br. Rufino's habits, went to the church in Assisi. When they entered, Brother Rufino was preaching about fleeing the world and giving up sin. Then St. Francis, himself naked, took over. St. Francis preached so powerfully about renouncing the world, turning from sin, and about the nakedness and humiliations that Christ had suffered on the Cross, that the whole congregation that day began to weep for their sins and was converted to an even deeper faith. God uses our folly if we humbly allow Him to do so.

We live today in a world that constantly bombards us with the message of how "worth it" we are. We deserve that nice meal, that big television, and that newer and more luxurious car. Don't the people in the commercials look "worth it"? Christ brings us a different message. It is not about us; it is about God first, and then it is about others next. We are called to be third and last. And Christ's message assures us of true happiness. This message was echoed in the writing of the late St. John Paul II who told the Church that the only life that was truly worth living was a life lived in the service of our brothers and sisters. It is not about us. It was never supposed to be about us. It was always supposed to be about our Lord and living His way. St. Francis had a very keen appreciation of that in his humility.

If we are really going to be Jesus's followers in this third millennium, we too have to be humble. May we also get out of ourselves. God can't be our God if we are too busy being our own little gods. We can humble ourselves, or God can do it for us. The choice is ours.

"Amen, I say to you, unless you turn and become like children, you will not enter the Kingdom of Heaven. Whoever humbles himself like this child is the greatest in the Kingdom of Heaven."

The Gospel of St. Matthew 18:3-4

"MESSAGES FROM ASSISI" - DISCUSSION GUIDELINE QUESTIONS

Chapter #2 - Humility

A. How is humility possible today? What does humility look like today? Why is it so hard to truly live a humble life?

B. Have you ever seen or experienced the fame and popularity that can come with living a holy life? How do we keep Christ first, when everything around is saying that we need to be number one? How do we remember how fleeting popularity really is?

C. How do we choose the "Little Way" in our own lives? Why is it important? How do we teach humility to our children and grandchildren in the world we live in today?

CHAPTER THREE

Friends, Community, And Church

"Hold nothing back of yourselves for yourselves."

St. Francis of Assisi

It should come as no surprise to us that someone who was as social as St. Francis was before his conversion would still value his relationships and the people around him following his conversion. Now, in the light of his renewed Christian faith, St. Francis saw all his brothers and sisters as co-workers in the Kingdom of God. And there was such a particular joy when God would send a new brother to join the community of Franciscans. God's love flowed out from each new member, as each one brought with him the particular gifts and talents that God wanted the community to have. Each person that they encountered became one more possible answer to their prayers.

While he was discerning and listening to God for clear direction on what he was supposed to do next following his conversion, St. Francis spent a great deal of time alone. He wandered the hills around Assisi, visited neighboring towns, prayed in caves, went to minister at nearby leper communities, and helped poor priests with their dilapidated churches. He did this by himself, almost in a personal formation for what God was going to expect of him next. But once he had discerned the direction that God wanted him to go, within weeks his followers arrived to join his work. His first three – Lord Bernard of Assisi, Peter Catani, and Giles— were there nearly from the very beginning.

I want to consider how St. Francis' first companion came to be with him and how the two of them made a community. This story sets the stage for a community that is one day going to reach all around the world. According to the *Actus* account, the nobleman Bernard of Quintavalle, was watching Francis. Being one of the wealthiest men in Assisi, he no doubt had heard the gossip and rumors about the only son of Pietro di Bernardone, from whom he had undoubtedly bought fine cloth and material for his home and clothing. Unlike most of the others in town, Bernard was fascinated with the possibility that this was more than mental illness or youthful rebellion. "What if," Bernard thought to himself, "what if God really is trying to tell us something through this young man?" After observing for a short time, Bernard invited St. Francis to come to his home for dinner. Francis accepted the invitation, and so there was the town's newest beggar dining at the home of one of Assisi's richest inhabitants.

The conversation during dinner mesmerized Bernard. And as it came to the end of the evening, Bernard invited St. Francis to stay the night at his home. This would have been very common back then. It was not only an extension of hospitality, but also a way of keeping a wonderful evening going on longer. Bernard would have undoubtedly also have known that St. Francis was living "on the street" by this time, so there is also an aspect of charitable kindness to the invitation. What Bernard really wanted to know was how St. Francis would act when no one was watching. He gave him his very fine, very plush bed, which St. Francis accepted and climbed into at once and fell asleep. Bernard had thought that perhaps the saint would sleep on the floor, rejecting the comfortable bed. St. Francis certainly appeared to be sleeping, even snoring, so that after a while Bernard himself fell asleep. Not long into the night, Bernard awoke to an amazing sight. St. Francis had gotten up and knelt down beside the bed, and was in deep prayer with God. St. Francis kept repeating over and over "My God and my All!" "My God and my All!" This did not last for a short time; it continued throughout the night. As Bernard listened intently and saw the devotion on the saint's face, his soul was changed by how real St. Francis' faith was. Bernard realized, as he heard St. Francis pray "My God and my All" that the prayer was not what God meant to him. And he prayed that from that moment on, he, like St. Francis, would be able to pray that humble prayer with all his heart. When the night was past, and the saint and Bernard spoke again, Bernard was a changed man. He wanted to follow St. Francis in way of complete and total love and abandonment.

St. Francis was wise enough to suggest further discernment, so they went off to a nearby church to have the priest read scripture for them. Three times, the Scriptures affirmed Bernard's decision. The first, from Matthew 19:20, were Jesus' words to the rich young man, that if he wanted to be perfect, he "should go and sell all that he had and give the money to the poor." The second, from Luke 9:3, was from Jesus's own instructions to his disciples about taking nothing with them on the journey, "neither walking stick, nor sack, nor bread, nor money, and do not bring an extra tunic." And then, as if both St. Francis and Bernard weren't amazed enough at God's words for them, the final opening was to the passage of Matthew 16:24, "If anyone wishes to be my follower, let him renounce himself, take up his cross, and follow me." St. Francis and Bernard prayed in thanksgiving and asked for the priest's blessing. And then the nobleman, Bernard of Quintavalle, went back to his fine home and gave away everything that he owned to the poor and needy in the Piazza del Commune.

St. Francis would say that Bernard of Quintavalle was the real saint who started the order, for it was he who followed the Gospel dictate and actually gave away ALL that he had, so that he could completely abandon himself into the arms of Christ.

Bernard was the first, and there were many others who came soon after. Giles, Philip, Silvester, Elias, Simon, Leo, Juniper, Masseo, Ruffino, and several others were among them. It is said that St. Francis had twelve original companions, just as our Lord did. Indeed, there are comparisons that are striking, including the fact that St. Francis, like Jesus, had one of his original twelve followers fall away. Brother Giovanni di Capella left the order. This was a sobering reminder to all of the original Franciscans that the Franciscan life was not easy, and many would not be able to complete it. According to the *Actus*, it is said that Brother Giovanni eventually would hang himself, just as Judas did.

It is amazing what Christianity fervently lived out allowed the Holy Spirit to accomplish! Some of Assisi's best and brightest (and most wealthy) were renouncing their former lives and going outside the town's walls to live as beggars with St. Francis. They were as a family. The care and devotion that they showed to each other was touching even to those who came to visit. Many of those who experienced this love, this piety, this true faith and devotion to the crucified Christ and to His Holy Mother, wanted to be part of it. It was contagious! One can easily see the seeds of the Poor Clares. It was quite natural really, almost demanded, that a similar group of sisters for women be founded. For that, St. Francis would later turn to a close friend. But the Franciscan life and spirituality was taking off like a wildfire, ready to set the Church ablaze.

What we also realize today is that for us to even survive in the world that we are living in, we've got to have fellow Christians around us, helping us to stay Christian. We cannot live this life alone; we were never expected to do live this life alone. We need God, and we need to know that. But we also need to know that we need each other. We are all not going to be running out to join a religious community. Although there are days all of us would probably love to run off and join the Franciscans, that simply isn't possible for the vast majority of us. (By the way, the Franciscan Third Order movement for the rest of us, is a way to be connected to this remarkable order. Check it out.) And yet all of us still need community. In our families, in our neighborhoods, in our parishes, and even in our dioceses, we need to be there for each other. That love that was so much a part of attracting people to the early Franciscans still has to be evident in our communities today, or else the shown compassion is not going to be real and authentic.

Isn't that one of the sad consequences of the breakdown of marriage and family, the impersonal neighborhoods we live in today, and in some cases even the massive parishes that we attend and belong to? It is harder than ever to be a genuinely loving community. I think that St. Francis has something really powerful to say to all of us today about sharing our faith together. It means so much more! And it is not an option. That's not from St. Francis. That's from Jesus Himself, Who called us to live together in peace and love in community! We've got to be better at this. We've got to get out of ourselves long enough to see the good that we can do for others. And we need to realize that working together and with God's Holy Spirit, we can do absolutely anything! Look at what God did with St. Francis, and Clare, and Bernard, and Masseo, and Giles! Nobody ever would have believed that what was at first thought to have been so crazy would eventually change all of them and our Church.

Take the time to care! Make that phone call. Send that e-mail. Mail a card or stop by and make that visit. Give that gift or share that treat. We have no idea the affect that we can have on others, or when God really is sending us as messengers of His love and hope to those who need us. And sometimes those who need us most aren't in Africa, or South America, or Haiti, they are living in the same house as we are, they are living next door to us, or they are praying in the pew right in front of us at Mass on Sunday. We don't need a brown robe to love God's people as St Francis did. We don't need Brother, or Sister, or Father, or Bishop in front of our name, we just need to be like Christ! And that, my friends, is something that we can all do!

Let us treasure our communities, all of them! My fear is that too often we take them for granted. And look what happens in a marriage if one spouse goes too long taking things for granted! That's when things fall apart. We forget what we are supposed to be for each other, and then pretty soon we simply aren't the people that we are supposed to be. St. Francis helped people, all people, reconnect with that. We don't get to choose our community, any more than we got to choose the families that we were born into. Our job is not to pick and choose; our job is to love. Sometimes the person who your love will mean the most to and whose life will forever be changed by your love are NOT the people that you would expect.

As a young diocesan priest, I was profoundly shocked after my ordination to realize that there were so many of my brother priests who were so needy and in need of healing and ministry. At one point, I remember saying to a close friend, that I could spend all my time as a diocesan priest ministering to other priests. I think it would drive me crazy, but the need is that great. As an immature young man, I told myself that that was somebody else's job, that it was the Bishop's responsibility, or the Vicar for Clergy role. I was wrong; it was my job. It was my responsibility! We are to love and care for WHOMEVER God sends our way! Stranger, different from us, not someone that we would be particularly fond of in another situation — it doesn't matter! That's who God sent to you at that moment! Accept the gift. Take up the challenge. St. Francis did that whether it was a leper, or Clare, or an upset greedy parish priest. God told us to love one another as He loves us. No exceptions. That's the way to be community!

"They devoted themselves to the teaching of the Apostles and to the communal life, to the breaking of the bread and to the prayers. Awe came upon everyone, and many wonders and signs were done through the Apostles. All who believed were together and had all things in common."

Acts of the Apostles 2: 42-45

"MESSAGES FROM ASSISI" - DISCUSSION GUIDELINE QUESTIONS

Chapter #3 -   Friends, Community, and Church -

A. Why was it so important to Jesus that we have other Christians around us? What is it exactly that the community is supposed to do for us? Why can't we do Christianity alone?

B. The primary role of the Christian community/the Church is... What? What is it that we have an obligation to do for one another in the Church? What is it that our souls most need from our brothers and sisters in the Church? How important is it to have friends who share the Faith?

C. What makes a good Christian community? How could our communities today be better? Why today is it not enough to just go to Mass once a week and "say" our prayers to be Catholic?

D. Several of the saints were hermits. How do hermits fit into the community? Why can't all of us be hermits? Wouldn't Christianity be easier if all of us went off to the woods to live in huts by ourselves?

CHAPTER FOUR

Conversion

"Sanctify yourself and you will sanctify society."

(St. Francis of Assisi

S t. Francis's conversion didn't happen all at once. The wealthy cloth merchant's son, the former prisoner of war, the recovering sick young man, was searching for something. He must have had a million thoughts racing through his mind. Not quite willing to give up his dream of knighthood and military glory, St. Francis left home once again to go to war in 1204. This time a local count was putting together an army to go and fight for the Pope Innocent III in southern Italy. Pietro Bernardone must have supported this new venture because he bought Francis brand new armor and a powerful new horse for the occasion. As with St. Francis's last experience with war, this one didn't last long either. Nearing Spoleto, scarcely a day's ride from Assisi, St. Francis met a poor knight who was coming back from war. The soldier was in bad shape. St. Francis, moved to great pity for the man who had already proven himself in battle, gave him his new armor and his new horse. This, of course, left young Francis with very little, other than the clothes on his back, and it changed his outlook and prospects for this journey and new adventure.

That night St. Francis had a dream. He saw himself in his father's warehouse, and it was filled with military weapons of every sort. Then he saw a magnificent castle with a lovely bride. And it was revealed to St. Francis that the castle, the bride, and the warehouse full of weapons were all going to be his. St. Francis's interpretation of this was that he should still move forward with his plans to go to southern Italy: God would take care of him. And in the end, there would be much glory and riches for him and his house. The next night, a second dream or vision clarified things a bit more. The voice asked, "Is it better to serve the lord or the servant?" St. Francis responded, "The lord of course." "Then why would you serve the servant?" the voice questioned. St. Francis woke up and asked God, "Lord, what would you have me do?" The voice told the saint to return to Assisi where he would be told more.

Now, going back to Assisi was going to be humiliating. St. Francis had already failed at military life once; now he was coming home after only a few days, minus his horse and armor. Certainly everyone, most especially his father, would think that he was a coward and a fool. Humility and humiliation was a central part of his conversion all along.

The Francis that returned to Assisi was a different man. He spent much more time alone; he stayed out in the Umbrian countryside. He started frequenting these small, run-down churches that were everywhere at that time. His search for answers and what God wanted him to do next eventually led him to go on a pilgrimage to Rome. When he returned to Assisi, he was visiting the remains of the little church of St. Mary of the Angels, down the mountain from Assisi. Here God continues the conversion of our saint. God had revealed that St. Francis would have to change his life. "All those things that you have loved and desired in this life up to this point, you must now despise and hate," the revelation challenged him. Leaving St. Mary of the Angels, St. Francis got on his horse and headed back up to Assisi. He had not gone far when he noticed a leper coming towards him on the road.

Now St. Francis, before he was SAINT Francis, despised lepers. He feared them; their look, their smell, and their situation repulsed him. It would have been Francis's normal response to get off the road and travel around where the leper was, in order to get back to Assisi without any contact with the sick man, even it meant traveling miles out of his way. But that's not what Francis did this time. The message from the little church had affected him. Francis took off at full gallop directly toward the leper. The poor leper must have been terrified hearing the approaching horse and not knowing who was coming or what would happen to him. It must have crossed St. Francis's mind to go right on past the man. But that's not what he did. He pulled the horse to a stop, dismounted, and went immediately to embrace the leper. Then he kissed his hands, or what was left of his hands, and then he kissed him on the mouth. And that singular act, that encounter, on the road between St. Mary of the Angels and Assisi, changed many things. St. Francis's fear was gone; he was on a new path. Christ was more present to him than ever before.

All of these things lead us to San Damiano. St. Bonaventure records another pivotal moment in the conversion of St. Francis, where Christ appeared to St. Francis on a Cross, and from that moment on, the Crucifixion was forever carved into St. Francis's heart. But what all biographers and followers of the saint recognize as the final transformation of Francis was his prayer at San Damiano. San Damiano was another little church just slightly down the hill from Assisi. It too had fallen on hard times and was a mess. St. Francis had been there before to pray. On this particular day, not long after the incident with the leper, Francis was praying in front of the Cross of San Damiano. Now this was an icon from the eastern tradition. When the corpus from the painted wooden crucifix spoke to him, St. Francis saw the lips of Jesus on the Cross moving. This is hard for us as twenty-first century believers to hear and imagine. We'd like to say it was an "inner" voice, or God spoke to his heart, or to the "depths of his soul". But that's not the tradition that has been handed down to us. St. Francis saw and heard the Crucifix speak to him. And he would never be the same again; St. Francis was a new man, a new creation in Christ. And from this moment on, nothing would ever be the same again. Conversion is always on-going. St. Francis was being converted more and more to Christ until the evening that he left this earth. But what happened at San Damiano took things to a whole new level. And there would be, and could be, no turning back.

God has an amazing way of converting all of us. You want to

hear some amazing stories, ask your friends who are real people of faith to share with you THEIR conversion stories. It makes for some very interesting conversations. God is much more real than we like to imagine. St. Francis knew that. And if we're honest, so do we. God has changed us if we have given Him that chance. And the other thing that is sure is that God is NOT done changing us. If we're living and breathing and still in this world, then God is NOT done with us yet! I have an old priest friend of mine who says that maybe, maybe…, fifteen minutes after we die we'll be done with conversion. If you're not dead, and you're a follower of Jesus Christ, then you'd better be ready to change.

It is certainly worth noting here that St. Francis' conversion was dependent on three very important things: his humility, his willingness to go beyond his fears, and his dedication to prayer.

St. Francis could easily have said, "No, Lord, it's going to be too hard for me to go back to Assisi in shame and face my father and my neighbors again after failing as a knight. I'm not going to do it." It would have been most of our reactions to what God was asking Francis to do. But St. Francis recognized that there was something bigger going on here than just him. Far too often we don't recognize that. And then our pride and our selfishness get in the way of real conversion for us and for others. We need to all approach God in absolute humility asking Him more and more what we can do for Him. He will tell you. He'll let us know. But only a humble heart is going to be able to listen and to respond.

Secondly, St. Francis faced his fears, his prejudices, and his dislikes head-on, and he was given a whole new perspective. That leper in the middle of the road was the perfect test from God. How many perfect tests do we get every day that we fail because we are unwilling to see things in a new light? That leper became Christ for St. Francis! How many times every day is Jesus waiting for us to recognize, or to minister to Him, or to love Him, and we don't because of our fears, our prejudices, and our lack of love? Conversion demands that we change our perspectives. We can't change if we keep seeing things always in the same old ways. God asked St. Francis to change his perspectives and he did, and everything was different after that.

Ask the leper! How many people do you think kissed him that day? And I'm pretty sure that St. Francis's embrace and kiss changed him too. It was not what the leper expected from some rich kid from Assisi. Sometimes we all need to change our perspectives.

And finally we talk about conversion all the time. There are more books and articles and homilies written about conversion than ever before. We all say that we want to be "converted" to Christ. As Christians that is our number one goal. What's the problem? We are sitting back waiting for conversion to happen to us, like it was a flu bug. It doesn't work that way. You want to be converted? You want to be more like Christ? Hopefully, if you're reading this, that is at least one of your goals. You must get down on your knees and pray! Or get yourself to the nearest Adoration Chapel. Or get out that old family Bible of yours that you are so proud of, and actually read it and pray it. The Book of Psalms is the perfect place to start. You can't read the Psalms with your heart and NOT be changed. Conversion is NOT automatic, folks! You must pray. That's why St. Francis was always stopping in those little churches. It wasn't to see the art. It was to pray. The more he talked to God, the more God talked back to St. Francis. And look what happened!

St. Francis of Assisi was always thinking about conversion. How could he be more Christ-like? He was passionate about it. The more he became like Christ, the more he mirrored his image. St. Francis so sought God in his life and was in fact so given over to God, that after a while that was all that people could see. St. Francis showed God to the Church and to the world at the beginning of the thirteenth century. The world was starving for God. Isn't it much worse now? And isn't it up to you and me to bring Christ to our world today?

"All that matters is that one is created anew."

Galatians 6:15

"MESSAGES FROM ASSISI" - DISCUSSION GUIDELINE QUESTIONS

Chapter #4 - Conversion -

A. Think of the greatest moments of conversion in your life, and ask yourself what exactly did you do to make that moment happen? What did you do afterwards to keep the conversion moving forward? Perhaps what didn't you do following your conversion moment that you should have done?

B. True on-going conversion is supposed to be the goal of every Christian. What can we do to persevere in our conversions, rather than to get stuck at one place, or even fall backwards in our growth as Christians? What do we do when we "backslide"? Hint: Just like Apple has an App. for everything, the Catholic Church has a Sacrament just for this!

C. The very best thing that you have ever done to help your own conversion process was... What? Are there specific actions/ activities/ and opportunities that can lead all of us to deeper conversion? How can we help one another?

D. How do you learn to be patient with God when you're in the middle of on-going conversion? What does patience with God look like when you're waiting on Him?

CHAPTER FIVE

Discernment

"Where there is inner peace and meditation, there is neither anxiousness nor dissipation."

St. Francis of Assisi

You don't have to look very far into the life of St. Francis following his conversion to see that discernment— the turning to God for guidance, help, and answers— became very much a part of his life, his ministry, and his spirituality. God was very real to St. Francis. St. Francis always desired to do God's will and to be in line with God's will. St. Francis became an excellent listener, but he was not a perfect listener, which is a good lesson for all of us, too. Even in interpreting the message of the Cross at San Damiano, St. Francis was off-target. But what is true of all real discernment is that the more that you do it, the better you become at it. St. Francis got much better at it as he grew even closer to God.

One of my favorite stories of discernment from the life of St. Francis is recounted in the *Actus* about how St. Francis made Brother Masseo twirl around. One day, in the early days of the order, St. Francis and Brother Masseo had set out to do the work of the Lord. They were traveling through Tuscany and came to an intersection in the road where a choice had to be made. At that one point, they could choose to go to Siena, Florence, or Arezzo. Brother Masseo, having reached the junction first, asked St. Francis where they should go that day. St. Francis responded, "We shall take the road that God wants us to go." And "How shall we know which?" Brother Masseo asked. St. Francis said, "I'll show you." Then, under holy obedience, St. Francis ordered the saintly Brother Masseo to spin around in circles like a little child. Now because this was such a popular intersection, many people passed by, and St. Francis allowed his brother to keep spinning for a long time. Many people had a good laugh at the sight. Brother Masseo was soon starting to get dizzy, but he trusted in what St. Francis was asking him to do, so he just kept going around in circles. After a long while, St Francis burst out with "Stop!" "Which direction are you facing?" asked the saint. "Siena," replied Brother Masseo. And off to Siena they went.

Now today, we think it somewhat humorous that one of the greatest saints of the Catholic Faith would discern in such a way. Why didn't he go into a church? Why didn't he kneel down in prayer? Why didn't he turn to Sacred Scripture, as we know he had done many times before, as was evidenced by the conversion story of Brother Bernard? The truth is that there are thousands of different ways to discern and to listen to God. St. Francis knew many of them. In everything he did, he was listening to God. And even when he got it wrong, he had the opportunity to go back to God. The greatest thing about discernment is that if we know that we have heard the wrong thing for whatever reason, and there are many, we can always go back to Him and start over. In fact, one of the first lessons of discernment is that if you have discerned wrongly, then be honest and humble enough to go back and find out what God was really saying. More than likely, you will even be made aware of why you discerned wrongly, and that there was some purpose, some lesson, even in that! That's how amazing our God truly is!

In the case of St. Francis and Brother Masseo's journey to Siena, when they finally did arrive in that beautiful town, St. Francis and Brother Masseo walked straight into what we would describe today as a civil riot. Two men had already been killed, and it was looking like many more were going to die in the fighting. St. Francis walked straight into the middle of the conflict, prayed, and preached to them about living together in peace and unity. The result of St. Francis's preaching and the people's great love of the saint was that the fighting and unrest stopped at that very moment. Who knows how many countless lives were saved because the fighting didn't resume that day? Brother Masseo marveled at this, as he remembered how close they came to not even going to Siena that day. And Brother Masseo marveled at both how God works and St. Francis's ability to discern.

It is strange how we as believers in the beginning of the twenty-first century don't turn to discernment nearly as often as we should, even as a Church. We set-up planning committees, and feasibility studies, and do research polls, but many times we fail to listen to God. Our prayer is not meant to be a one-way line of communication. Our God wants desperately to talk to us and for us to listen to what He has to say because He is trying to get us home to Heaven, and because He wants our passage through this life to be as peace-filled and joy-filled as possible. God has so much in store for us, not just in Heaven, but right now! We've got to be better at listening!

The early Church discerned everything. They asked God to guide them on what to do next, where to take the Gospel next, who was to be sent out as missionaries. St. Paul's writings are full of stories of a Church that discerned everything that it did. What happened to that trust in the Holy Spirit? Discernment keeps us focused on the fact that all of this is God's work and God's kingdom. Once again it is NOT about us. We as Church are not supposed to be nearly as practical as we are supposed to be Spirit-filled and trusting in a God Who is very real, even in the twenty-first century!

We should take all things to prayer; every decision should be taken to God. God's guidance is there for us in big things and in small things. And like St. Francis, the more we discern, the better we get at doing it! If we get used to discerning daily for our actions and decisions, then we will be much better at it when it comes to our vocations, our jobs, our marriages and families, and our places in the community.

We try and discern everything within our Parish family. From our parish council to who's going to be in charge of our parish festival: it is all discerned. The more we do it, the more all of us get used to doing it, and I think we are getting better at it. Discernment demands three things: faith, humility, and honesty. Let's talk about these three things...

If we believe in a living and true God, and we say so every Sunday in the Creed, then we must trust in His way for us and seek that way every day of our lives. We even say would that the more we line our lives up with God's will, the happier and more peace-filled we are going to be. Certainly, the life of St. Francis of Assisi also bears witness to this truth. Re-read his conversion story again, if you have doubts. If this is all true, then we have to have faith not only when we are talking to God, but even more so when we are listening to God.

There are thousands of different ways to listen to God, but all of them start with prayer. We ask for God's guidance and help, and He shows us the way. This happens sometimes in little quiet ways. And many times it happens in big, loud, dramatic ways. But if we're not listening with our hearts and souls, sometimes we can even miss the big and dramatic ways if we're not tuned in to what God is trying to tell us. Discernment demands a complete trust in God. We can't be afraid. Fear is sometimes the devil's best tool. We have so many people in our world today who are so afraid of so many different things. If you're going to have faith, you can't be afraid. If you're going to be afraid and let fear rule your life, then where is your faith? We as God's children have NOTHING to be afraid of. God has taken care of it all. Do you have enough faith to let God lead you every day, in every thing that you do? And if not, how could you increase your faith so that you could allow that?

The second thing that true discernment demands is humility. We can't let God guide and direct our lives if we are too busy trying to be our own god. There is a reason that the First Commandment is "I am the Lord your God; you shall not have FALSE gods." It is because it is our number one sin! When we seek to discern God's will for us, we must humbly acknowledge that God knows the best way for us and that we want to be in line with His Holy Will. And we must be willing to do whatever God asks us. Sometimes it is going to sound crazy. Just imagine what Brother Masseo must have been thinking as he was spinning around like a little child at that intersection that day! Sometimes we've got to be willing to spin around a little bit and trust God. If He's going to bring good out of it, who cares how silly we look? The goal is goodness and holiness. Discernment is not about us. Sometimes, you know, we get to thinking that we have to do this or that we can't do that, because of our stature in life. That's called pride. It is the opposite of humility. And nothing kills our ability to listen to God quite like our pride. Take a step back. Put God first. Get out of the way and let Him take you to real glory! Isn't it strange how we seek so many honors and so much esteem for ourselves, when the Little Poor One of Assisi gave all of that up, and today is more glorified than any other person who walked the face of this earth, with the exception of Jesus and Mary? St. Francis put Jesus and Mary first in his life, and God did the rest. St. Francis didn't have to do another thing or say another thing. God had him covered. Do you trust that God has you covered too? And then can you let go of worrying about yourself?

Finally, discernment also demands honesty. Too often today, even within the Church, we trade honesty for being "nice." We're not honest with one another. We want everybody to like us. We live in the age of political correctness. And so we're "nice" to each other. We don't want to ruffle any feathers; we don't want to judge. This usually is about what we don't say, rather than harsh words that we do say. We apparently really listened to our mothers when we were growing up, and bought into that "If you can't say anything nice, don't say anything at all" message. The problem is that sometimes the Gospel demands that we speak up and tell the truth. Today the truth of the matter is that there are souls going to Hell because we are being "too" nice. St. Paul says that we are to always "speak the Truth with great love and charity." And if we can't be honest with one another, then it is far too easy to also not be honest with God. It just doesn't work at all with God Who knows our hearts. If we are trying to discern anything, and we're not being honest with God or honest with others or even honest with ourselves, it is NOT going to happen. We are not going to hear God in the middle of "part of" the truth. We've got to trust God and each other enough to be honest. Let me assure you, some day, God is going to be very honest with all of us about our lives. Before we get to that day, let's start being honest with ourselves, with others, and with Him. When we're honest, we'll know His will and discernment will be oh, so much easier in our lives.

Our prayer and discernment also affects God, His will, and even the discernment of others. The *Actus* also recounts the story of St. Francis and one of his companions being very kindly received into a good man's home. St. Francis was so impressed by the man's hospitality, love, and goodness, that when they left his home, he commented to the brother traveling with him that the man should be one of their order. St. Francis said, "That gentleman certainly would make a good member of our order; he is so grateful to God, so kind to his neighbor, so generous to the poor, and so cheerful and courteous to guests. For courtesy, dear brother, is one of the qualities of God. I have observed so much divine virtue in this good man." The saint desired to return to the gentleman's home soon to see if God had worked on his heart. A few weeks later, they did return. Shortly before arriving at the man's home for the second visit, St. Francis stopped to pray not far from his home. He prayed fervently that if it be God's will, that God would call the good man to leave the world and join him and his order. The man saw St. Francis praying so devoutly from his home. And while he didn't realize that St. Francis was praying for him, the sights of the saint's holy prayer inspired the man to run out and greet him, informing St. Francis that he immediately wanted to join his order. Sometimes you have to watch who's praying for you and what they are praying for you to do!

The true fruit of discernment is peace. It is as simple as this, if you want a more peaceful life, start discerning everything. Once you experience the peace that comes along with living in line with God's Holy Will, you will realize that you can't live without that deep, deep peace. It's what our hearts and souls were made for. Indeed, I'd have to say that the greatest thing that a life of faith can offer us, when we are living in God's will, is that deep peace. If everybody knew what God is offering us right now, when it pertains to His peace, our churches would be full and everybody would be Catholic Christian. St. Francis tasted that peace and knew that he could not live without it. It was that intoxicating. God's peace is more powerful and more fulfilling than things, than money, than sex, than popularity – and it lasts forever while all of these other things of the world are passing away. Put your trust in peace. Seek that peace every day.

Let God's peace permeate your heart, your soul, and your very being. That's why we need to discern. St. Francis had it down. That peace spread like a wildfire in his heart, in his order, and through him to our world. Are you a messenger of peace? Does Christ peace rule your heart? Or do you just shake hands on Sunday at Mass, and that's the extent of your "peace"? God offers so much more!

"If God so clothes the grass of the field, which grows today and is thrown into the oven tomorrow, will He not much more provide for you, O you of little Faith? So do not worry and say 'What are we to eat?' or 'What are we to drink?' or 'What are we to wear?' All these things the pagans seek. Your heavenly Father knows that you need them all. But seek first the Kingdom of God and His righteousness, and all these things will be given you besides.

The Gospel of St. Matthew 6::30-33

"MESSAGES FROM ASSISI" – DISCUSSION GUIDELINE QUESTIONS

Chapter #5 - Discernment –

A. Why is it important that we as Catholic Christians learn to discern? What does it offer us? Can you think of examples from the Bible of people discerning God's will? What's the value of it?

B. Certainly, St. Francis was frustrated several times in his discernment of God's will. How can we avoid frustration? How do we persevere even when we don't feel like we are getting an answer?

C. What about when God's will is radically different from our own will? How do we find the courage to change our hearts, our minds, and our lives, when they are clearly not where God is leading us? How did St. Francis do it? What can he teach us about responding to discernment?

D. What's the toughest thing that God has ever asked you to do? Did you eventually find peace about the change? Maybe why haven't you found peace with the change? And what would it take? If you have found peace, what did you do to enable that to happen?

CHAPTER SIX
Obedience

> "Live always in the truth that you may die in obedience."
>
> *St. Francis of Assisi*

sk any priest, bishop, sister, brother, or deacon in the Church, and they will tell you that the hardest vow that they took when they received Holy Orders or entered religious life is the vow of obedience. It's a funny thing, too, because it is usually not the one that you think is going to be most difficult. I can remember as a seminarian, both at St. Meinrad College Seminary in southern Indiana and also as a graduate student at the North American College in Rome, being so concerned about the vow of celibacy. Many hours at both places I spent on my knees in front of the tabernacle asking God for the grace to live up to the vow of celibacy. I wanted to take it very seriously, and I did. Such was where a young man's mind, heart, and body were in those days. If I could go back to that time and concentrate on only one vow, I would have spent much more time praying about obedience—the giving up of one's own will to the ascent of the Will of God. The difficulty, of course, is never in God's Holy Will; the problem always shows up when under the vow of obedience, you have to be obedient to those in authority that God puts over us: our superiors, our spouses, our parents, our bosses, our teachers, etc. That's when the vow of obedience becomes real, and we have to give up what we want to do or even what we think best, and do what we are bound by obedience to do. And that can be the hardest thing for any of us… bishops, priests, deacons, religious, married folks, even single brothers and sisters… to live up to and to live out our lives obediently.

St. Francis of Assisi could understand and relate to this completely. He too knew the "dying to self" that has to happen if he was to be truly obedient to God. Throughout his conversion process and in the early days of his ministry *il Poverino* knew that he had to get out of the way and God had to become everything in his life. From the moment that St. Francis decided to really, completely give his life to God, he knew that it couldn't be any other way. But that "dying to self" sounds so final, so romantic, and so easy when you read about some saint doing it. It is a different thing when it is your own will, your pride, and your sense of control that has to be beaten down for God's will to be done.

There were still very challenging days following the Crucifix speaking to St. Francis at San Damiano. St. Francis did rebuild the church at San Damiano, and then the one at St. Mary of the Angels, which would become his favorite, and he worked on several other little, poor churches in the area. He continued to work with the lepers and begged for food for them nearly every day. And all during this time he lived essentially as a hermit, in deep prayer and contemplation, striving to do the will of God.

God would eventually lead St. Francis back to Assisi and to the confrontation that he most wanted to avoid: facing his father. The now infamous account of Pietro Bernardone confronting his son Francis in the piazza near the bishop's house, was not what St. Francis wanted, but it was the way that he knew that it must be. And so St. Francis the "son" strips himself of his clothes, his sonship to Pietro, and his own wants and desires in order to give everything to God.

And isn't that what obedience to God really is? It is an abandonment; it is a giving up and giving over to something bigger than we are. It is facing our fears, and our doubts, and our concerns and still trusting in a God Who we certainly don't always know or understand. And yet that abandonment becomes the most supreme act of trust and faith, opening us up completely to what God has in store for us next. Those are easy words to write on a page of paper. And yet actually doing that leaves us standing there, sometimes just like St. Francis, naked in front of a lot of people who are already judging us. Francis of Assisi became a saint of God because he learned how to get out of the way. Perhaps there is no better lesson that he offers to us at the beginning of the twenty-first century than how we too can and need to do the same.

The *Actus* gives us another wonderful story from the early days of the Franciscan Order, when Brother Leo taught St. Francis another kind of lesson in obedience. At that time, the Order was so new and so poor that the brothers didn't even have books to use to pray the Divine Office. St. Francis and Brother Leo got up to pray matins. St. Francis said, "Brother, we spend this time praising God. I will say something, and then you must say exactly what I tell you, careful not to change my words. I will say this: 'Brother Francis you have done so much evil and sin in the world that you deserve hell.' - and you, Brother Leo must answer: 'It is true that you deserve the depths of hell.'" And Brother Leo who was very pure of heart and obedient to God and to St. Francis replied, "All right, Father, let us begin in the name of the Lord." Then St. Francis began to say, "Oh Brother Francis, you have done so many evil deeds and sins in the world that you deserve hell." And Brother Leo answered, "God will perform so much good through you that you will go to Paradise." "Don't say that, Brother Leo!" St. Francis responded. "When I say: 'Oh Brother Francis, you have done so many wicked things against God that you deserve to be cursed by God,' then you answer this way: 'You certainly deserve to be placed among the damned.'" And Brother Leo replied, "All right, Father." Then St. Francis said aloud, crying and sighing and beating his breast, "Oh, my Lord God of Heaven and earth, I have committed so many evil deeds and sins against You that I deserve to be utterly damned by You." And Brother Leo answered, "Oh, Brother Francis, God will make you such that you will be remarkably blessed among the blessed." St. Francis wondered why Brother Leo would not answer him the way that he was told. And so he scolded him, saying, "Why don't you answer as I tell you, Brother Leo? I command you under holy obedience to answer what I tell you. I will say: 'Oh wicked little Brother Francis, do you think God will have pity on you, for you have committed too many sins against the Father of mercy and the God of all consolation for you to deserve any mercy.' And you, Brother Leo, Little Lamb, Father, because I will say just as you tell me." And St. Francis, kneeling down and lifting his hands toward the Lord and looking up to Heaven with a joyful expression, said very sadly, "Oh, Brother Francis, you great sinner – oh you wicked Brother Francis, do you think God will have mercy on you, for you have committed so many sins?" But Brother Leo answered, "God the Father, whose mercy is infinitely greater than your sins, will be very merciful to you and moreover will give you many graces." At this reply St. Francis was gently angry and patiently troubled, and he said to Brother Leo, "Brother, why have you dared to go against obedience and to have already answered so many times the opposite of what I told you?" And then Brother Leo exclaimed very humbly and reverently, "God knows, dear Father, that each time I have resolved in my heart to answer as you told me, but God makes me speak as pleases Him and not as pleases me." St. Francis was amazed at this and said to him, "Brother, I beg you to answer me this time as I tell you." Brother Leo replied, "Go ahead, in God's name, for this time, I will answer as you wish." And St. Francis cried out, weeping, "Oh wicked little Brother Francis, do you think God will have mercy on you?" Brother Leo answered, "Yes, Father, God will have mercy on you. Besides, you will receive a great grace from God for your salvation, and he will exalt and glorify you for all eternity, because 'whoever humbles himself shall be exalted' – and I cannot say anything else because God is speaking through my mouth!" The *Actus* says that "they stayed up until dawn in this humble contest, with many tears and great spiritual consolations." We always have to listen to God.

In various ways St. Francis learned to not only listen to God, but to obey Him. St. Francis found a new freedom in belonging to God, in trusting completely in His ways, and in total abandonment to whatever the Lord wanted. Obedience became for St. Francis a sacred thing, a necessary thing, if he was going to stay close to God. First and foremost *Il Poverino* expected that of himself. He knew his sinful nature, he knew his inmost thoughts and desires, and he knew very well how far away from that God that he so desired he actually was. That's why the saint demanded such a strict, at times even severe, obedience to God for himself. Desperately desiring sainthood and sanctity for each one of his brothers who came to join him, and eventually the same for the sisters who joined St. Clare, unquestioned and complete obedience was demanded of those who came to follow in his footsteps. St. Francis knew that after he was gone, they would need to carry on the message and the work in fidelity to the spirit of the Order that God had shown him. How could St. Francis ask his brothers to be obedient to God and to himself and the Order, if he himself were not also obedient and faithful?

Today those in any kind of authority would do well to pay attention to St. Francis's concern. Too often today, we want authority, we want to be in charge, and we want to make decisions. And when we are given even a little bit of authority, we forget that if we want others to respect our authority, then we must also respect the authority that is over us. And all of us are under many different kinds of authority. We can't ask those under our authority to respect us, if we don't show at least the same respect to the authority that we owe allegiance to. I have seen this so much today with parents. Parents always want their children to respect their authority. And yet in so many cases today, parents don't respect authority themselves. They unknowingly teach their children to disrespect authority. And then when the children get a little older, in their pre-teen or teen years, and have no respect at all for the authority of their parents, then mom and dad scratch their heads and wonder what happened. In fact, they themselves planted the seeds of disobedience themselves for many years in the child's life. St. Francis knew what he was talking about.

In our culture and society today, obedience is seen as almost a "dirty" word. Too often it is associated with "oppression" and "submission" and "slavery". The very real virtue of obedience is under attack today. The radical feminist movement and also the radical gay and lesbian rights movement despise the word "obedience". And they have both sold all of us a bunch of lies to make themselves feel good about what they are doing or want to do. They see obedience as repressive. That's not the way that St. Francis or any of his followers saw obedience. In fact, the saint would tell us that nothing frees us more than being obedient to God! Simply put, it works! Oh, if only we, with our "modern" minds and polluted points of view, could see and understand what St. Francis was talking about, maybe we would all be a whole lot happier and more at peace.

That's still not to say that obedience is always easy, even for saints. There is a story about St. Francis that takes place after the saint had had his conversion and began his ministry, but before anybody else had come to join him. It is mentioned several times in nearly all accounts of St. Francis's life, how very important it was to him that a candle be kept burning in front of the crucifix in churches. This started at San Damiano. It became a priority for St. Francis to keep the priest supplied with oil for the lamp, so that it would never go out. This of course calls to mind our modern sanctuary lamps in our churches today that are kept burning in vigil by our tabernacles. St. Francis actively begged for money for this oil and in many cases for the actual oil itself. On a particular occasion, when a priest had indicated that they were nearly out of oil, *Il Poverino* went out at night, and observing that one house was very well lit up with lamps, he put two and two together and realized that would be the perfect household to ask for help with oil. If they had that many lamps burning, surely they would have a large supply of oil. As St. Francis approached the house, he could see in the windows. And when he looked in, he realized that it was a gathering of his former friends. In fact, a couple of years earlier, St. Francis himself would have been in that room with those exact same people with all the lamps lit. St. Francis's pride kicked in and he could not walk into the middle of that group begging for oil. They knew too much about him; he was too close to them. It would be humiliating for him AND for them. St. Francis, in his compassion, was acutely aware of how uncomfortable it was going to make his former friends gathered in that room to be put in the position of having to help their former friend and party-goer. Nearing the door, St. Francis turned around and walked away. It was better for all that he ask someone else for the oil, he reasoned. He did not get more than a few feet from the door, when he realized that he had to go back and knock on that door out of holy obedience. It was God's work that needed to be done and that oil was needed for that lamp in front of the crucifix. It didn't matter how uncomfortable he was or how uncomfortable it made his former friends, St. Francis HAD to knock on that door and beg for oil. It wasn't about him or them. It was only about God and what God needed from at that particular point. What a tough thing to do! How much easier it would have been to go to the next house!

How many times do we take the easy way out, rather than obey what God really wants us to do? And we are experts at making excuses. There's always an excuse not to do the right thing, not to do what God wants us to! And we know them all. And if we don't know them, the devil is oh, so good at providing them for us in our heads at the exact moment that we most need to do God's will.

We need to stick with the truth. The Bible says that the Truth will set us free. How can we not obey a God Who knows infinitely more than we do? Just like with humility, it is entirely about getting out of ourselves and letting God be God in our lives. My advice? Try it. Just give God the chance. Give him one month of doing things His way. Just see if you're not happier, and more at peace, and more fulfilled, living according to God's will than what you were living by your own wants, desires, and appetites. I'm promising you that God will win the challenge! Try it. I dare you!

"My son, if you receive my words and treasure my commands, turning your ear to wisdom, Incline your heart to understanding."

Proverbs 2: 1-2

"MESSAGES FROM ASSISI" - DISCUSSION GUIDELINE QUESTIONS

Chapter #6 - Obedience -

A. There is perhaps no word in our vocabulary with more negative connotations than "obedience". Why are we so afraid of being obedient? Why does our 21ˢᵗ Century society so abhor obedience?

B. St. Francis' obedience both took him many places and also cost him dearly. And yet, even when he was wildly popular and clearly a living saint, St. Francis was still obedient to Franciscan superiors that he clearly disagreed with on some fundamental principles. How does pride affect obedience?

C. Who is a positive example of obedience today in our world? Who is a poor example of obedience in our world today? Don't we need good examples of obedience to be obedient ourselves?

D. How can we see God's will in obedience to those that He has put in authority over us? What happens and what do we do when those in authority over us aren't in accord with God's will? Can't authority all too easily be abused? And what about obedience then?

CHAPTER SEVEN
The Love of the Cross

"Brief is the world's treasure, but the punishment that follows it lasts forever. Small is the suffering of this life, but the glory of the next life is infinite."

St. Francis of Assisi

You don't have to read or study very deeply into the life, spirituality, and faith of St. Francis of Assisi to realize that the Cross of the Crucified Christ is central to everything for him. At Spoleto and San Damiano, at Santa Maria degli Angeli and Alverna, the consistent meeting point between Jesus Christ and His servant Francis of Assisi, was the Cross. It would be only here that St. Francis would experience a God Who is NOT dead, but who is very much alive, and Who loves His people even unto suffering and death. St. Francis would take this a step farther and say that it is when God becomes our all, when He is all that is left that genuine conversion takes place. Not only our natural physical deaths, but also our spiritual dying to ourselves that takes place within our souls is demanded. When we become lesser and lesser, and like St. John the Baptist, He becomes greater and greater. Through his life, his conversion, his ministry, and his order, and eventually through his own death, St. Francis experienced God so intimately in the cross that that is where Jesus came alive for him. The Passion of our Lord on the Cross was exactly where God most showed His love for all of us. St. Francis felt that love deeply in his heart. The

Crucifix, any crucifix, was a constant reminder of God's love. The saint would weep merely passing by a crucifix. It was as though the crucifix melted his heart and reminded him of what real love is.

How very different from our experience today! Today we run from crosses. We pray that we won't have them, or that they won't be too big. The crucifix is fine for those three hours on Good Friday afternoon, but why in the world would we want to dwell on the Suffering Christ for very long? The cross scares us. We've been to nursing homes, and oncology units, and funeral homes. Modern man can find very little to love about the cross. Instead, frequently we blame God for our crosses, thinking that somehow He doesn't understand what we go through. In actuality, it is the exact opposite. If anyone should be blaming anyone else for crosses, it should be God blaming us. We create crosses the minute that we as human beings decide that our way is better than God's way. We forget the words of the Gospel that tells us to pick-up our cross and follow Him. And there simply is no way of following Him without the cross.

Perhaps there is no greater lesson that *Il Poverino* can teach us than a love for the Cross of Jesus Christ. Yes, the cross involved suffering and even death, but the cross was the instrument of salvation. Christ's saving action on the cross redeemed mankind and opened the possibility of the gates of Heaven for all of us. For St. Francis, it was much, much more personal than that. It was the Cross of Jesus that taught St. Francis an entirely new way of looking at life and living as a son of God. In particular, in identifying with the suffering of the poor, and with an intimacy with them and their plight, St. Francis found new meaning and new faith. For the saint, everything was turned upside down. This radical poverty, this extreme penance and self-sacrifice in conjunction with the Cross, brought an incomprehensible joy and peace to the saint's life and the lives of his followers. It was radical. It flew in the face of everything that the world taught and believed 800 years ago. And guess what? It certainly flies in the face of everything that the same world throws at us every single day. The cross only makes sense with great love. St. Francis had experienced that great love in a deep prayer that most of us will probably never achieve. St. Francis loved Jesus Christ, especially Christ Crucified.

What St. Francis would also tell us is that real love only makes sense, and can truly only be real love, with the cross. The cross was the only way to Jesus AND the only way to Heaven.

Later, the receiving of the stigmata would further unite St. Francis and our Lord in the cross. And ultimately, frail and weak, blind and lame from his sufferings and penance, St. Francis would deliver over his soul to Jesus Who was raised from the dead. St. Francis was dying. He was going home to a complete union with God that he had so much desired all his life.

I am acutely aware that for most of us it is right here where we start to draw the line. We can listen with a certain fascination, even admiration for St. Francis, but when we really get a taste of what *Il Poverino* is trying to tell us with the cross and about the cross, here's where we put St. Francis of Assisi over there, and ourselves over here, and we think that there's no way we can be like him. It's not true! We can be like him. But we can't be like him if we don't really embrace the real cross, the whole cross. It was Pope Pius XI who was writing about St. Francis when he said, "The herald of the Great King did not come to make men doting lovers of flowers, birds, lambs, fishes or hares; he came to fashion them after the Gospel pattern, and to make them lovers of the Cross." This is a drastic call back to reality for all of us who love St. Francis, who seek to know more about his way, and who want to follow him to Jesus. We romanticize this saint so much more than any other. We are fascinated by the little charismatic man in the brown robe; we are forever enamored by his joyful poems and songs, by his talking to the animals, and by his extraordinary preaching that had such a powerful, moving effect on so many. The legend, the miracles, and even the stigmata all fascinate us, even 800 years after his death. We have this happy, positive, romanticized image in our heads that only reveals to us half of the story. There's much more to St. Francis of Assisi that isn't as comfortable or as easy to handle. St. Francis was, as Pope Pius XI said, primarily a "Lover of the Cross." St. Francis was about the Crucified Christ; to him it was everything. He was a preacher of the Gospel of Jesus Christ, and that Gospel was centered on the cross. He didn't just preach it. He lived it.

We don't like to think about the freezing nights outdoors with little more than rags to protect him, the real hunger pangs when there was no food, or the dirt, the stench, the lice, the rats, or the nothingness that comes with true poverty. So many of his modern biographers have deliberately left out tales of his great penances, from going for weeks without food to punishing his body until he bled, or his inconsolable weeping over the passion of Christ throughout his life, or the great personal cost of trying to keep the order that he himself founded on track and true to its origins especially in the last years. Our sunny, happy idealistic holy card image gets shattered when we get real with St. Francis. I think that was what Pope Pius XI was talking about. St. Francis' love and faith were as radical as Jesus' love and faith. We can't forget that especially when it comes to the cross. St. Francis wanted us to be "lovers of the Cross". Not social workers, not ecologists, not animal-rights activists, not just soup kitchen volunteers, but lovers of the cross. It seems to me that we've really got to get that right as Church.

What St. Francis had discovered through his conversion process was that it was truly the love of God revealed in His Son Jesus Christ, which was lived out, or even played out, on the cross. Christ had sacrificed everything, holding nothing back, to demonstrate His love and the Father's love for humanity. Jesus' actions in His Passion and death forever changed everything about the way that we live in this world. Now, with Jesus's cross, there is a real power in every sacrifice that is made. From our big sacrifices to our most miniscule, insignificant choosing of our lesser options, God can, will, and is doing incredible things with every sacrifice that we make. St. Francis saw this in such a tangible way. He would wear the habit with the most holes and stains. He would eat the last, oldest and most stale piece of bread. He would sleep on the hardest and most uncomfortable spot on the ground. And in his choices, the more he sacrificed, the more he embraced the Cross, the more powerfully alive in his life God's love became. We, like St. Francis, are given so many opportunities every day to embrace the cross: by giving another preference in traffic, by choosing the lesser portion, by not complaining about a given situation, and even by accepting what we have as enough. Our sacrifices of our cross not only simplifies our lives, but it gives true meaning to our love and service. For as St. Francis found out, real crosses and true sacrifice have got to be much bigger than words and nice ideas. A real love of the cross has got to be lived out in our actions.

In so many ways, our cross can be our ladder out of this world. The cross raised up St. Francis' perspective of what this world and what this life were all about. St. Francis firmly believed that Jesus had a different and unique perspective high on that cross, nailed up there above everything else. The cross also allowed St. Francis to have a whole new perspective that changed everything and put many things into their proper perspective. Our sacrifices are extremely important. Today we need that same new vision more than ever in our lives and in our world. We don't hear a call to the cross much on TV, or the Internet, or certainly not in our advertising. If we the Church aren't showing a new way through the cross, then we can be sure nobody is.

One day, for all us, we are going to get that one cross that is going to take us home. For some it will be a long burdensome cross of cancer or Alzheimer's disease. For others it may be a brief excruciating accident or heart attack. But our final cross, our Cross of Calvary, is coming one day for all of us. We'd better be making our peace with the cross and with our Savior Jesus Christ now. The cross is not a bad thing. God has changed all crosses forever with what He did on One Cross outside of Jerusalem. May we not be afraid. May we let our crosses change us into the people God needs us to be today. Everybody gets crosses. It is entirely about what we do with them and how we help others to carry theirs.

"ONE WHO DOES NOT SEE THE CROSS OF JESUS IS NOT SEEKING THE GLORY OF JESUS,"

St. John of the Cross

"MESSAGES FROM ASSISI" - DISCUSSION GUIDELINE QUESTIONS

Chapter #7 - The Love of the Cross

A. Why in your opinion was Francis Bernardone so affected by the cross? Of all parts and symbols of Christianity, why the cross? What did this rich young man know of the cross?

B. What is the crucifix's connection to love?

C. How do we learn and teach to our children the notion of sacrifice and embracing the cross in the middle of a society and culture that so rejects the very notion of sacrifice?

D. How can we help one another <u>not</u> to be afraid of crosses? Where does our faith come into play when dealing with crosses in our own lives and in the lives of those we love?

CHAPTER EIGHT

The Craziness Of It All

> "The Lord told me that He wished me to be a new kind of simpleton in this world and He does not wish us to live by any other wisdom than this."
>
> *St. Francis of Assisi*

The closer that St. Francis got to Jesus, the more people there were who said he was crazy. Pietro Bernardone, his father, was the most obvious. But there were many other relatives, old friends and acquaintances, and many others from the town who knew the family who all said the same thing: "Isn't it too bad about the Bernardone boy!" The saint had gone too far, they thought. He had crossed over some invisible and undefined line of what was reasonable, what was practical, and what was within the boundaries of normal, even for holy and pious people. Other holy people didn't take their clothes off in the piazza in front of the Bishop's house, or sleep in caves and run-down churches in the countryside, or beg for food and rocks from their former neighbors. And it was easier for everyone to handle what St. Francis was doing when they could chalk it up to mental illness - a disturbed mind. To really have to deal with Francesco Bernardone's new way of life, his giving everything away, and his radical and complete reliance on God, was too much! That's why it was so much easier to dismiss St. Francis when he was starting out. He's just crazy. Gradually the people's opinions did change somewhat. But when they started to hear about some of the miracles, and when several other, very reasonable and even upstanding people from the community of Assisi went off to join him in his new way of life, and when what St. Francis was doing proved to be more than a passing whim or a temporary cause, it became much less easily dismissed as crazy. Then they had to deal with what St. Francis was saying and doing.

St. Francis's new way of life didn't make sense. The way of St. Francis was radical; it was no-holds-barred Christianity, taking the Gospel to its most radical and most literal extreme. For St. Francis, Jesus wasn't messing around in the Gospel stories. He meant what He was saying when He talked about not worrying about what we were to eat or drink, or about giving away all our belongings to the poor, and about living completely on Divine Providence. Jesus was trying to teach us, His followers, His Church, this new way of life. In the time of Christ, it was also true that many didn't understand what Jesus was saying or doing. There were, in fact, good reasons why they hung Jesus up on that Cross on that first Good Friday. If they had understood more of what He was trying to do and teach, maybe things would have gone differently. But Jesus was radical. He was different. No doubt that there were those in 1st Century A.D. who also firmly thought that Jesus was out of His mind. Jesus was a real threat to them and to their world. You don't crucify nice, harmless, itinerant teachers. Make no mistake about it, Jesus scared them to death. St. Francis would tell us that in his time, in the twelfth and thirteenth centuries, the radical, gut-punching power of Jesus's Gospel had all but completely been removed from Jesus's message. Even the Church was paying lip service to Jesus's radical call and challenge. St. Francis of Assisi heard so much more when he listened to and read Scriptures. Jesus's words were so real to him that they struck at his very heart. St. Francis couldn't stay the same. At the beginning of the thirteenth century, St. Francis was exactly what the Church and the world needed. Certainly to the world, but in many ways also for the Church of that day, what St. Francis was doing and preaching did seem crazy. And yet how desperate were both for his extreme faith! And how much more does the Church at the beginning of the twenty-first century need to hear the radical interpretation of the saint from Assisi!

Today in the Church we are so practical and responsible. We do feasibility studies and invest wisely. We have so many committees that our sub-committees have sub-committees. We have forms and certificates, and we document everything! We're good stewards; at least that's what we tell ourselves in an age when we hear so much about stewardship. We hear the Gospel every Sunday. We have book shelves full of books on the Gospel message. It's all so safe and secure and accepted. The Church has been preaching the Gospel for almost two-thousand years, we say. And sometimes it really feels and seems like it. Unfortunately, there is NOTHING crazy about the Gospel in this twenty-first century. We've heard it all before. And much worse, those in the world around us think that they too have heard the Gospel message all before. It's like a re-run on TV. We know what to expect and how it is going to go. Eight hundred years ago, St. Francis unsettled a very settled Church with his new experience of Jesus. And they thought he was crazy! We romanticize it away today, as though there was simply some breakdown in communication, as though somehow they just didn't understand or get it. "They sure were wrong about St. Francis, weren't they?" we say. "But didn't he look good in his tattered brown robe?" Today we think that we can recognize holiness by the way it looks. And yet if St. Francis appeared in our time saying the exact same things as he did 800 years ago, even wearing the same thing as he did 800 years ago, my guess is that we would all be right there with those who knew him in saying he is crazy. He should be locked up. I don't think I want my kids hanging around this guy. Isn't it really time that we let his experience and message also unsettle us? When was the last time anybody thought that anybody in our Church today was crazy? It's been too long. Maybe we ought to be worried about that.

Of course, the joy that we started out this discussion with didn't help matters much. How was it that St. Francis and the early Franciscans were so happy and joy-filled? Well they must all be crazy! You can't possess nothing and be that happy. You can't have to beg for your food and other needs and still have a smile on your face. You can't wear those scratchy robes, and have those funny haircuts, and not bathe and still be joyful. Unless...unless you are crazy. Insanity takes care of all the questions, doesn't it? Why did that guy try to kill President Reagan? He was crazy. Why did that young man blow-up the Federal Building in Oklahoma City? He was angry and crazy. Why did those two students shoot up their high school at Columbine? They were bullied and crazy. They must have been, no, they had to have been CRAZY! However, people who do bad, terrible things aren't the only ones who are crazy. Sometimes crazy people have smiles on their faces! Sometimes they go to church, and pray, and wear robes! For a long time it was easy to dismiss the Franciscan way of life as crazy. But as the Franciscan way of life grew and spread and St. Francis' message truly began to change the Church, what was crazy then? Who was crazy? And the real question that they had to face, and perhaps the biggest question that we have to face today, is if this guy is crazy, then why, oh why, does this little man from Assisi seem to know something that the rest of us do not? He sure seemed a lot happier than everybody else.

Now, it is worth pointing out that we still have to use our heads. God gave us brains for a reason. And while many things about our faith lives will never make sense or be reasonable, we together as Church do have to be responsible and smart and accountable for what God has entrusted to us. It's just that when our logic or our responsibilities or our intellects keep over-riding what we know and feel in our hearts and souls, that's when we stifle the "craziness" that God so needs! God's logic and wisdom is always much better than our own anyway! We would do much better to do things His way, as St. Francis did, and figure out the "how's?" and "why's?" later on.

Maybe it is time that we all got a little crazy for Christ! It is not always going to make sense. The radical nature of the Gospel is going to open us up to the charge of insanity, especially if we are really doing Christianity the way that we are supposed to be doing it. This would be especially true if we could be less serious about ourselves, and more open to the infinite power of God. So St. Francis preached to the birds, and talked to a wolf, and hugged a leper, and cried in front of crucifixes, and made his companion preach in his underwear. It was all a little "out there" as we would say today. Let's be honest, it was more than a "little" out there. It was a lot out there! And yet, when you put it all together with the other-worldly perspective that this extraordinary man had, both of God and of God's world, it all made perfect sense. The world was and is crazy. St. Francis knew that; St. Francis had it right all along.

At some point early on in his conversion process, it simply quit mattering to St. Francis what other people thought. St. Francis felt more alive and in touch with reality than ever before. He was at peace. The pieces of his life were finally fitting together, not by wealth or popularity or status, but by being a little crazy, a little out there, for God. Everything came to matter. Nothing was created on its own, and nothing had meaning on its own. All of creation was working together for the glorification of God. If some folks, even many folks, thought that he was crazy, that wasn't what mattered. St. Francis knew that he could live without acceptance or affirmation or even support. And he also knew that he couldn't live without God. He needed God like he needed the air he breathed. A little humiliation was a good thing, for St. Francis knew well the warning from the Gospel about the dangers of everyone speaking well of you. He was happy to be a "fool" for Christ.

Oh how much better off we'd all be if we'd just get that right ourselves! What if we worried less about what everybody else thought and were more concerned about what God thought and saw in us? What if we weren't afraid to do the right thing, no matter how crazy it might seem? Wouldn't we enjoy life so much more if we weren't concerned about appearing foolish or crazy? So dance, and sing, and shout, and laugh, and cry, and make funny faces, and enjoy the incredible creation that God has provided us while we are in this world! Because it is all just a preview of the Kingdom that is to come!

Are those Catholic Christians crazy? You bet we are! Sanity is over-rated anyway.

"For God's foolishness is wiser than human wisdom, and God's weakness is stronger than human strength."

1 Corinthians 1:25

"MESSAGES FROM ASSISI" - DISCUSSION GUIDELINE QUESTIONS

Chapter #8 - The Craziness of it All

A. Does Christianity really look less "crazy" today than it did a hundred years ago, five hundred years ago, a thousand years ago? How do we keep our "edge"?

B. Does the radical nature of St. Francis' life and teaching excuse most of us from his challenging interpretation of the gospel message? Are we "off the hook" because we aren't that radical?

C. St. Francis' radical new lifestyle forever changed his relationship with his family and many of his friends. Would God really want us to lose or damage our relationships to that same extent?

D. How do you know when you've crossed "the line" with religion and faith? Can you be too "crazy"? Is there a point where we are doing more damage than good?

CHAPTER NINE

The Sacredness Of Our Time Together

> "For what else are the servants of God than His singers, whose duty it is to lift up the hearts of men and move them to spiritual joy."
>
> St. Francis of Assisi

The Actus, and its Italian translation, *I Fioretti*, recount a story about both Saints Francis and Clare that I also think has a great deal to teach us today. When St. Francis was in Assisi, it was his routine to stop by San Damiano and check-in on Clare and her sisters. Many times he and Clare would have powerful spiritual conversations that fed both of their holy souls. St. Clare was greatly consoled with his holy advice. She was very grateful for his visits and the time that they shared. At one point, St. Clare suggested that at some time, they might have a meal together. This suggestion was made more than once. Yet St. Francis, who never wanted to appear to have favorites, or perhaps even to give in to something that he himself might really enjoy, refused to accept St. Clare's invitation. His companions noticed this and, knowing St. Clare's great desire to share a meal with him, they questioned his refusal and suggested that he grant her request. After all, Clare was "holy and dear to God". In addition, they reminded him that it was at his preaching that Clare gave up the "riches and pomp of this world".

St. Francis eventually consented and the meal was set up. It was to take place at St. Mary of the Angels, where St. Clare had her hair cut off and where she made her first vows to St. Francis on that Palm Sunday evening several years back. St. Clare brought with her one of her sisters from San Damiano, and St. Francis asked one of the brothers of his community to accompany them. The other brothers gathered around them, and they sat down on the ground to eat their meal. As the first course was served, St. Francis began speaking about God and the spiritual life in such a holy and marvelous way that both he and St. Clare, and both of their companions, and indeed all who were sitting near them, were mesmerized by his words. Their hearts, minds, and souls were lifted up to God. And together they praised God for all the good that He had done. While this holy group was praying through the course of their evening meal, the townsfolk of Assisi looked down in the valley toward St. Mary of the Angels and saw a strange light all around the place. They assumed that the holy church and community buildings of the early Franciscans were on fire! And they ran down the mountain to help put the fire out. When they arrived, they found St. Francis and St. Clare and their companions still in rapt prayer, the glow of which filled the entire forest. When the saints "came back to themselves" as the *Fioretti* states, they were so completely spiritually satisfied that they had little hunger for the material food that was before them. St. Clare was escorted back to San Damiano, where her sisters were waiting to hear how the meal had gone.

I suppose we wonder what it would be like when two saints get together, most especially these two saints. And yet St. Francis and St. Clare's evening together that night reminds all of us of the sacredness of our time spent together and most especially of the sacredness of sharing a meal. This is something that we are losing. Some would say that we have already lost this practice in our society today. I recently read an article that was lamenting that the average American family now eats all together only three or four times a week. Different schedules, work, sports practices, drive-thru, take out, and microwave ovens have all taken their toll on family life and so many of our relationships. This is so true for all of us. I have to admit that even at our rectory, it is nearly impossible to get priests and even seminarians all together for meals. The work load is such that most evenings, we work right through the evening meal time, and straight into that magic hour of 7:00 PM when all things Catholic start at local parishes. All of us fail to make time to have meals together. It is because it takes a coordinated effort on everybody's part that so many times we don't make time to be together period. This is dangerous for families, marriages, friendships, and pretty much all households, all relationships, and all communities. We need our time together! And so often we don't get it.

As a diocesan priest, the standard reply is that if you want community and companionship, then you should have joined a religious community. First of all, I know religious communities that are struggling with this same problem. A Franciscan friend of mine told me recently that he can go for weeks without seeing some of the guys that he lives with. Secondly, don't all of us as human beings simply need each other, and when it comes to the spiritual life, wouldn't we all be better off if we shared our faith more with others? For anyone to suggest that the only way to find that kind of support and interaction is to join a religious community, seems pretty extreme to me.

When is the last time that you and the people that you are close to, had a serious conversation about God, or about what God is doing in your life, or about being one of His followers? We don't talk near enough about all these things. And that's too bad. We need to support and sustain and build-up one another in our faith. You would be amazed at what another's story from their walk with Christ can do to you. And certainly most of the time, we have way too little appreciation for the profound effect that we can have on others. We have the ability in every single encounter of every single day to raise up the soul of another. I think that must have been exactly what St. Clare was hungering for with St. Francis. We all need this kind of sharing and interaction for our souls. It doesn't have to be at mealtime, but it has to happen some place and some time, and why NOT at a meal? What do you talk about when you sit down at table? What did you talk about at the last meal you ate? Why is it that we find it so much easier to talk about the weather, or the latest sports scores, or the latest gossip at work, than we do to talk about our faith? Our faith is at the very heart of who we are. Are we afraid of revealing too much? Or have we simply lost the art of conversation? I worry about this very much with our young people. It seems far too often the minute that we ask them to turn off the computer game or to take off the I-Pod, they don't know what to do or what to say. But it's not just our young people; it is all of us. They just have neater toys. We are all losing the art of conversation.

St. Francis had a remarkable ability to be in the moment with whomever he was with at the time. He wasn't concerned about the past, and he knew that there was not always going to be a future. And no matter how busy he was, he would never pass up an opportunity to share an encounter with someone and have the opportunity to witness to Christ. It was certainly one of the things that St. Clare and so many others most enjoyed about him. He was completely present to them, whether that be to a leper on the road or to St. Clare at St. Mary of the Angels.

Wouldn't we be a whole lot more respectful of one another if we were more like him? Our time with one another is sacred. It is a gift from God. We never know how much time we will get with friends and loved ones. But what we do know is that it is not forever. We need each other. It is the way that God created us. And we need to have healthy, spirit-building conversations to help each other to be better. St. Francis wasn't afraid to have conversations about God. For he knew that by sharing our faith in this way, that we are actually building one another up and passing on our faith to others. Funny, we think religion is one of those topics best NOT to talk about in polite conversation at the table. Isn't religion right up there with politics and money? It might make someone "uncomfortable". And while St. Francis might agree with that about unbelievers and people of other faiths, when did Christians, especially Catholic Christians, stop talking to each other about our faith, a faith that is supposed to be the thing most central to our lives?

A few years ago I was in restaurant after a movie with friends of mine. I don't recall what the movie was, but I know that it led us into a conversation about martyrdom and the holy martyrs of the Church. About an hour into the conversation, an older couple who was sitting next to us came over, and asked if they might be able to join us for the rest of conversation, as they were really enjoying "listening in". St. Francis knew that people wanted to talk about these things. These are the things that are going to last! We can talk about the weather, or the latest movie, or how our favorite NASCAR driver is doing this year all we want; it just isn't very fulfilling. It is not very substantial. We can't be afraid to have substantial conversations, for by them hearts are changed.

I was talking recently with an older friend who was telling me that the thing she longed for most in Heaven was the time and opportunity to have real, substantial conversations with loved ones in God's Kingdom. She said that now she has so many things that she would like to talk to her parents, grandparents, and great-grandparents about. Unfortunately, we know all too well the things we would like to have said and talked about with departed loved ones. Likewise, she said it will be so nice to be able to talk to friends, children, grandchildren, and neighbors without anybody having to rush off to their next thing. I truly believe that my friend, like St. Clare, was hungering for good conversation, even holy conversation. I am sure that she is right and that we will find it in Heaven. Maybe until then, and to help all of us to get to Heaven, we ought to be having more holy conversations right now. My friend's words really touched me. I try to call her a little more and stop by more often, and I try to spend a little more time now than I can usually afford. I haven't regretted any of it because the words that have been shared between us have made all the efforts worth it. There's a life and a faith wisdom that is meant to be shared and passed on and discussed. Both St. Francis and St. Clare knew this. They knew how powerful our words to each other can really be.

Perhaps one reason why we don't have more conversations about our faith and about the things of God is that so many of us feel like we don't know enough to have a decent conversation. We know that in the Catholic Church, the majority of Catholics are trying to live out their faith with about a sixth- grade level of religious education. St. Francis would be the first one to encourage all of us to learn as much about our faith as we possibly can. Sometimes before we can share faith, we've got to know it ourselves. There are so many excellent books! If most of us had even the slightest inkling of the vast treasure that was out there in great Catholic literature of all types, I know that we would spend the rest of our lives with a good book in our hands, or at least always beside us. Many parishes and communities are offering all sorts of really excellent adult education programs, but what is the most common cry all over the world, not just in the Church, in the U.S.? It's that it is always the same 20 or 30 people who show up for every adult religious education offering. Why is it that we can be so good about demanding that our children and our young people attend religious education, but somehow think that as adults WE don't need it? We can always learn more. We've got to keep feeding our soul. The more we feed our soul, the more we are going to have to share with others. Maybe with more information we will be less afraid to talk about these important things in life.

So...make time to get together! Eat more meals together as a family and friends. Talk about more important things the next time you get together with people that you care about. Talk about your faith more the next time you get together with brothers and sisters in Christ. I think you'll enjoy it more than you might imagine. When is the last time your conversation with others "glowed"? Maybe that should be our goal too.

"Father, they are Your gift to Me. I wish that where I am they also may be with Me, that they may see My glory that You gave Me, because You loved Me before the foundation of the world."

John 17:24

"MESSAGES FROM ASSISI" - DISCUSSION GUIDELINE QUESTIONS

Chapter #9 - The Sacredness of Our Time Together

A. What do you think is the greatest obstacle that we face in building solid faith relationships with others? Are our faith relationships different from our other relationships? How do we make true Christian friends? Is that important?

B. Have you ever had a holy conversation? What made it holy for you? Did it make you desire to have more conversations that lifted up your soul?

C. Where do you find your support in the Christian life? Is that support something that you actively seek out in your life? Is it really possible to find that kind of support in others?

D. What do you think it was that St. Clare most needed from St. Francis in their relationship? And let's flip that around, what do you think that St. Francis most needed from St. Clare in their relationship?

E. Many of the saints knew each other, and at least a few of them spent a good deal of their lives together or in contact with one another. Does it help to become a saint if you hang out with other saints?

CHAPTER TEN

Taking The Message Out To Everyone

"Preach the Gospel always! Use words only when necessary."

(St. Francis of Assisi

St. Francis heard the powerful words of St. Matthew's Gospel 10:5-10 on the Feast of St. Matthew in 1206 or 1207. And with them he received his mission from God. The life of a hermit, and restorer of small churches, and care- taker of lepers was good and was rewarding. St. Francis knew that he was doing God's work and learning valuable lessons along the way. But St. Francis wondered if there wasn't more to "rebuilding the Church" that he was supposed to do. In fact, a question that seemed to haunt him at this time was whether should he go out to others to evangelize and share what he had learned about God, or should he just keep doing what he was doing in Assisi and the surrounding area? The message at Mass on this one particular day answered his question loud and clear. St. Francis heard the words of the Gospel with new meaning and a new sense of urgency. He went up to the old priest who had celebrated the Mass and asked him to verify what he had thought he had heard. When the old priest verified the message, it all became so much clearer for our saint. He knew exactly what he and his brothers must do for God. He would go out into the streets of Assisi, and Spoleto, and Perugia, and Siena; he would go as far as God wanted him to go. He would spread the message, and he would do so taking the Gospel at its every literal word, with a complete trust in God and God's generosity. And if St. Francis would need anything at all to do God's work, then God would provide it for him. St. Francis's strict adherence to the Gospel's travel advice is giving new definition to "traveling light".

Most importantly for St. Francis and his early followers was the absolute centrality and importance of evangelization and preaching. *Il Poverino*'s preaching would change everything. St. Francis firmly believed that you couldn't just preach with words, but that with every action, every moment, and everything that you did, you were either preaching the Good News of Jesus Christ, or you were preaching something else, usually yourself. By this point in his own journey, St. Francis had learned how to get out of the way and out of himself and let God be truly in charge. This became evident immediately to his listeners when he was preaching. St. Francis wasn't just saying nice words; he personified what he was talking about. His life and his lifestyle gave a definitive legitimacy to the Gospel that he was preaching. He preached as a man who had every right to be saying the things that he was saying, because he was completely living the Gospel message.

Thus St. Francis became a preacher that everyone - the poor and the rich, the powerful and the lowly, the young and the old – wanted to listen to and to hear preach. God had revealed exactly what St. Francis was to do and how he was to do it. He had prepared him well for the job beforehand. And when it became crystal clear what St. Francis and his band of followers were to do as their primary work, they knew they were to take Jesus out into the world again, every bit as much as the Apostles had done 1200 years earlier. Their identification with the poor, their complete adherence to Gospel values, and their ministry to the sick and dying would all give their preaching a richer and deeper meaning that would change hearts and change lives. And out they went. And from this point on, there was no stopping what God was doing.

This same message is also for all of us. Whether or not we have ever preached to anybody, and my hunch is that if you're reading this book, at some time, in some way, you have preached to others, we all need to hear St. Francis's challenge to us to evangelize. Far too often, we want to leave evangelization up to some committee at our church or in our diocese, or in our community, or we make a donation to buy some banners, or maybe we go around putting up flyers for some upcoming parish event, and we like to think that this is evangelization. And while those things and many others are important, isn't there a lot more to taking the Gospel out to others than putting up an 8 1/2"-by-11" piece of paper?

St. Francis got it right. Our lives are our homilies. We may never stand at a pulpit and preach in the traditional sense, but let me assure you, that all of us are either preaching Jesus Christ or else we are preaching something else. We must ask ourselves who our life bears witness to. Are we taking the Gospel out to others? Or are we just enjoying this life of faith for ourselves? And most especially in our world today, we need to authenticate and legitimize our message with our very lives. We must live out our faith. It's got to be so much more than just words for us, too. There is perhaps nothing that the world hates more today than a hypocrite. Christianity has long suffered more damage from our own members than any outside persecution or anything the world put in front of us. We've got to truly be Christians if we are going to dare to take Jesus's message out to others. Evangelization demands an accountability to God, to each other in the Church, and even to ourselves. And yet when we are truly following Christ ourselves, preaching and evangelization become a by-product of the life that we are living.

We as Catholic Christians love that Jesus in the tabernacle in our churches. We take great pride that He is there and we can turn to Him anytime that we want. But we have a terrible history of keeping Him locked up there, and not taking Him out to share Him with others. All four Gospels make it very clear that ALL OF US have a primary responsibility to evangelize and to take Jesus out to others. Evangelization is a Gospel imperative. It is not a choice or an option for anyone who follows Jesus Christ. Souls are being lost because we are NOT living up to our call and responsibility; we are NOT doing our jobs.

You know, when it comes to evangelization I think that St. Francis of Assisi would tell us to pray for courage. It does take courage to witness in faith. Let's be honest, it took courage for St. Francis to hug a leper, and to leave home, and to give away his possessions. St. Francis had to have courage and put his complete trust in God and God's providence when he first went out begging, when he accepted his first follower, and when he traveled on foot to Rome to ask the Pope for approval to start his new religious order. At so many times in his life and in so many very different ways, St. Francis had to be courageous. And his courage, even in the face of doubt with obstacles stacked against him, and in terrible, even dangerous situations, always allowed God to do some of His very best work.

We must remember the courage of St. Francis of Assisi every time we are faced with an opportunity to love and serve God by witnessing to our faith. Whether it is praying before a meal in a restaurant or talking about faith and our religion to someone who needs it, we need to be courageous! God will never abandon His people when they are doing His work. That's what St. Francis found out. And that led to more courage and more opportunities and more evangelization. The life of faith is all connected. We have a major role to play. We must evangelize to others, and in doing so, we will take our own faith to places and levels that we can't even begin to imagine.

St. Francis perhaps made his greatest difference with his preaching. Certainly, what started the rapid growth of the Franciscan Order was the preaching of St. Francis and his early followers. They were on fire for God. The Holy Spirit blazed in each one of them, and like any powerful fire, it spread, and it changed hearts, and it drew others to Christ and to what St. Francis was doing. You know today in the Church we talk all the time about vocations, usually bemoaning the fact that we as a Church don't have enough priests, sisters, brothers, and deacons. Do you really think if all of us, clergy and laity, men and women, young and old, parents and single folks, were evangelizing that we would still have a vocation "crisis"? I don't think so. I had a really disturbing conversation a few years ago with a lay person who worked for the Church in a position of leadership in religious education. She, with all frankness and candor told me that she refused to pray for more vocations in the Church today, because she knew if there were more priests, deacons, sisters and brothers, that she and people like her would be out of jobs and would lose their place in the Church. St. Francis would be appalled at this mindset and ecclesiology! I think he would really feel saddened that any daughter of God would actually feel that way. The Church is big enough for all of us! We've all got plenty of work to do. It is going to take all of us to build the Kingdom of God. But to not help others find what God wants them to do in that building process, all because we're trying to protect our own place, is suicidal to a Church community. What is that particular lay person preaching with her actions? I don't think it is the same thing that Jesus and St. Francis preached with their lives.

Let us take seriously then our challenge to take the message out to others. I am absolutely convinced that we have people starving for God out there. So many of our anxieties and psychological challenges can be traced right back to the fact that we have people who are so desperately missing God in their lives that it has impacted their mental health. They don't need another new outfit, or a new car, or more friends. They need God in their lives! We, like St. Francis, need to be ablaze for God! The Gospel message is so much more than nice words. It is the way for us to find peace, and happiness, and genuine meaning in each of our lives. God has so much more planned and in store for all of us than what we can even begin to imagine. Give Him the chance to show you exactly what He can do through you.

It does take courage to get out there and evangelize. Just like St. Francis, others will think you're crazy. They might think that you are a "Jesus Freak". They might think or even say that you are intruding into a very personal area of their life that you don't have a right to go into. But we can always plant seeds. Once we plant those seeds, we may never see the results of what we said or did, but God will. And others will also. If we are preaching and evangelizing like St. Francis did, with our whole lives, then others may still disagree with us, but they will admire the fact that our preaching is more than nice words.

St. Francis's fire and enthusiasm for his faith was so evident, but he never ever tried to beat anyone over the head with religion, or the bible, or the Franciscan way of life. He certainly never demanded the conversion of anyone. He simply told whomever he was preaching to exactly what he knew and had experienced of Jesus Christ in his own life, and let that be enough. It was Francis's friendship and love that so touched those he came in contact with. That friendship and love changed people's hearts, even some of the most hardened hearts, as we will see in Chapter 19 of this reading. A gentle approach can do a lot of good. It can change the world.

May the prayers of St. Francis help all of us to be better evangelizers and to take the Gospel everywhere today!

Jesus sent out His disciples with these instructions: "As you go, make this proclamation: 'The Kingdom of Heaven is at hand.' Cure the sick, raise the dead, cleanse lepers, drive out demons. Without cost you have received; without cost you are to give. Do not take gold or silver or copper for your belts; no sack for the journey, or a second tunic, or sandals, or walking stick. The laborer deserves his keep."

St. Matthew's Gospel 10:5-10

"MESSAGES FROM ASSISI" - DISCUSSION GUIDELINE QUESTIONS

Chapter #10 - Taking the Message out to Everyone

A. What's the best homily that you've ever given?

B. Today, what are the best ways to "preach without ever saying a word"? Can our message get lost without the right words? Can we be too quiet at times about our faith?

C. Where is the hardest place for you to witness to Christ? Is that possibly exactly where you need to start witnessing more? What would it take? Where exactly is God asking you to take the faith at this point in your life?

D. Where do you get Christian courage?

E. Have you ever met someone in your life that was "starving" for God? Has there ever been a point in your life where you would say that you were in that situation? What "fed" you? What or who was it that nourished you back to spiritual health?

CHAPTER ELEVEN

A Meeting Of The Brothers/ The Chapter Meeting At St. Mary Of The Angels

---

"I caution the friars and beg them not to look down upon or pass judgment on those people whom they see wearing soft or colorful garments and enjoying the choicest food and drink. Instead, each must criticize and despise himself."

St. Francis of Assisi

The *Actus* records for us the story of a General Chapter meeting of the Franciscan Order that took place probably in 1218. It is believed the *Actus* might be combining stories from at least a few General Chapter meetings, and putting them into one event. St. Bonaventure also records the story but places it a little later on, perhaps 1221. St. Dominic is said to have been present for this meeting. It is believed that St. Francis and St. Dominic, the two founders of the 13th century's great mendicant orders, met at the Fourth Lateran Council, which was convened in Rome in 1215 by Pope Innocent III. The Council was called to address the growing religious orders that would have a great deal to do with the Church getting better; both St. Francis and St. Dominic would have been invited by the Pope to attend the Fourth Lateran Council. St. Francis and St. Dominic both had great respect for each other and what the other was doing. Even with communication being very poor back then, both saints were accomplishing so much in such a brief period of time, that stories of their success could not have escaped reaching the other. It seems natural then, that when St. Dominic found out that St. Francis had called a General Chapter meeting of all the Franciscans at St. Mary of the Angels, and St. Dominic was traveling in Italy at the time, that he would go and see what his friend Francis was doing and what the Franciscans were up to. Also present at this General Chapter was Lord Hugolin, the Cardinal of Ostia, who was a great supporter of St. Francis and his order. St. Francis had rightly predicted that the Cardinal would become pope, and indeed later he was elected Pope Gregory the Ninth. It was a most impressive gathering there on the plain down below Assisi!

The early Franciscans had a tradition of gathering together once a year, with all the brothers coming back from all around the world. Perhaps this particular gathering was made even more special by St. Francis's personal interest in it and his desire to keep all of his brothers on the same path. It is said that over five thousand brothers arrived on the plain of St. Mary of the Angels. Huddled together in small groups, the friars were everywhere. There was such a great number of them that people of every walk of life came from all over to see the sight. At night, their small fires dotted the plain below Assisi. Cardinal Hugolin is reported to have stated: "Truly this is the camp and the army of the knights of God!"

When all of the brothers were present, St. Francis, who was considered by all to be the "holy Father" of the order, stood up to address them. With a loud voice and with the Spirit of God, St. Francis called his flock to maintain their sacrifices for God. Promising them that God had promised them much more than they had promised Him, he exhorted them to prayer, penance, and most importantly of all, poverty. He asked them to place all of their hope and trust in God. Then he said, according to the *Actus*, "In order that you may better observe this, by merit of holy obedience I command all of you friars who are gathered here that none of you is to have any care or anxiety concerning anything to eat or drink or the other things necessary for the body, but to concentrate only on praying and praising God. May you leave all of your worries about your body to Christ, because He takes special care of you." The multitude of brothers received this message with great joy and peace.

We know that by this time there was at least some level of dissention in the Franciscan Order on the importance of poverty. The *Actus* itself says that even St. Dominic, whose own order of the Dominicans was likewise bound by a vow of poverty, was very surprised by the extreme nature of what St. Francis was saying. St. Francis's words were undoubtedly challenging to everyone. How does one live trusting entirely on God for everything that he needs? Doesn't God help those who help themselves? The words are as challenging today at they were 800 years ago. Does God really want us to live this way?

Then God, as if to prove his servant Francis correct, gave the order a gift. He inspired men and women from every town in the area – Assisi, Perugia, Spoleto, Spello, Foligno, and many others – to bring gifts of food to His holy servants. They came from all over bearing gifts of bread, and beans, and wine, and cheese, and they brought everything that the Friars needed to have an excellent meal, even table service. God proved that He took care of His servants like no one else. The brothers were in awe of God and St. Francis, and they recommitted themselves to trust in God's Divine Providence.

It is said that this event and miracle had a great effect on St. Dominic, who apologized to St. Francis for second-guessing him. St. Dominic, like all who had attended the Chapter, left the plain of St. Mary of the Angels renewed and strengthened in his resolve to trust God and live entirely by His means and by what He provides.

Divine Providence scares most of us to death. We like to plan and prepare and worry. What if God doesn't give us something that we really think that we need? And yet there is no freer way of living than by trusting God for everything. If God doesn't give it to you, then you must not have really needed it. That day-to-day faith is exactly what all of us need more of in this life. You don't have to be a religious or a priest or even Catholic to trust in Divine Providence. It was what Jesus was talking about when He talked about God's taking care of the "birds of the air". You don't see birds with insurance policies, or storage units, or large bank accounts. Are we really sure that we need those things as much as they tell us that we do?

God is calling all of us to a simpler life. There is a great difference between what we think that we need and what we really need, certainly what God thinks that we need. We have an entire world now full of people who confuse "need" and "want" with remarkable dexterity. Our hunger for more, newer, larger, the latest, is killing us. At some point we've simply got to say "enough is enough" and re-examine our desires. St. Francis and his way of life points us straight back to Christ and to a much simpler way of life. God is interested in what we need. God also wants us to be happy. And yet God knows, and so should we, that our things are never going to bring us real happiness. The bigger, newer home, the more luxurious automobile, the latest style clothes, and the most technologically-advanced gadgets will never make us truly happy. The commercials and advertising are lies to get us to buy the latest products. Those companies are not interested in our happiness. They are interested in making more money for themselves. God is interested in our everlasting happiness. He's got a plan. He's got us covered. All we have to do is trust and rely on Him! And that, my brothers and sisters, is Divine Providence.

A few years ago, I was volunteer for Blessed Teresa of Calcutta's Missionary of Charity sisters at their home for the poor in Rome, San Gregorio. One night, a young Indian sister asked me to get her some blue thread from their storeroom in the basement of the home. I went downstairs and was able to come up with ten different shades of blue thread. There was sky blue, navy blue, silver blue, purple blue, and several others hues. When I took them upstairs and presented them to the sister, my efforts were greeted with, "None of these, brother, is the right color blue." Sister was looking for more of what we would call "royal" blue. I wondered what awesome piece of cloth that this particular royal blue thread was needed for that Sister was so specific? Was it a vestment for Mass, or a cloth for the chapel, or perhaps even for the blue trim on one of the sister's saris. Because sister was so specific about it, I even wondered if perhaps it was for Mother Teresa's own personal sari. Such were my dreams of glory. I asked, and she told me that it was needed to fix something belonging one of the men who lives on the street. I couldn't believe it. I knew the man and I knew his old blue jacket, and I knew that tomorrow he would probably leave it in some park somewhere. And yet, sister was so specific about the thread to be used to repair it! I was more than a little perturbed. But trying to learn humility and trust from the good sister, I marched myself back downstairs to the storeroom to put away the ten different colors of blue thread that were NOT good enough for a poor man's jacket. I was not in the lower level of the home for more than a minute, when the bell rang signifying a delivery for the sisters and for the home for the poor. This happened every so often. This particular night, Alitalia, the Italian airline, was dropping off their monthly donation to the poor. With Alitalia, you never knew what you were going to get. It could be blankets, or bread, or clothing. I opened the delivery door and helped the driver start unloading this month's donation. The very first box that I unloaded from that truck was a box of something like five-hundred spools of royal blue thread. It was exactly what the sister wanted and had prayed for. And God had provided for her in abundance. She could make that poor man several entire new jackets with all the royal blue thread that God had sent her. And I, still feeling like a heel and a heathen as I write this story down so many years later, was amazed that God cared so much for a young sister in a home for the poor in Rome, Italy, and for a poor man's jacket, and for a priest's faith, that He would give her exactly what she asked for in abundance in just minutes.

We know that not all prayers are answered in this way. But we are all called to have faith in prayer. If all of our prayers were answered in such tangible ways, it would be easy for everyone to have faith. But that would result in an on-demand summoning of God that is not faith. Trusting that God hears each and every one of our prayers and answers them according to His will is essential to faith.

We are all called to trust in God and in God's promises to all of us, not just people in brown robes with funny haircuts. Faith in Divine Providence can revolutionize the way that we live every day. We are so confused by our needs and our wants that most of us don't have any idea what we really *need* in this life any more. Doesn't everyone need a bigger TV? St. Francis asks us all to rethink our priorities and to let God have a chance. We can keep going the way that we are. We can keep pursuing everything and anything that we desire. But it is not going to make us happy. And it is not going to give us peace. We'd do well to recognize that fact sooner rather than later.

St. Francis knew just how incredibly well this works when we really live this way. He always knew that God would take care of him and his order, as long as they maintained this extraordinary trust in the Lord. Eight hundred years ago, there were plenty of doubters in Divine Providence too. Some of them were even members of St. Francis's order. And yet this very special meeting at St. Mary of the Angels seemed to ratify for everyone that God's generosity will never be outdone, especially to those who have faith in that generosity. How much do you trust in God's generosity? Do you trust enough to be truly generous yourself? We are called to be generous with our time, our talents, and our treasure. Are you sure that our God will never let us be more generous than He is? It is a matter of faith. It was for the early Franciscans, and it is for all of us today.

"For God's foolishness is wiser than human wisdom, and God's weakness is stronger than human strength."

1 Corinthians 1:25

"MESSAGES FROM ASSISI" - DISCUSSION GUIDELINE QUESTIONS

Chapter #11 - A Meeting of the Brothers / the Chapter Meeting at St. Mary of the Angels

A. Why was it so important at this time in the history of the Franciscan order, for the community to gather together? What did St. Francis most want to accomplish with this gathering? What does it teach us about our families and communities?

B. Why is it that more people don't live by divine providence? What are the challenges of living by a complete trust in God? What are the great benefits? How do we move closer to that kind of trust?

C. There are those who say that materialism is completely out of control in our society today. How do we not get caught up in a love of things? What kind of guards and protection do we need to put into place in our lives to keep us from the constant pursuit of more things?

D. Is the Franciscan life the only option in avoiding materialism? What else can we do? And how do we protect our children today?

CHAPTER TWELVE

Prayer

"Idleness is the enemy of the soul, therefore the servants of God must always give themselves totally to prayer or to some good work."

St. Francis of Assisi

There is more written today about prayer than at any other time in our history. And perhaps, since you are reading a book about spirituality, you might expect that somewhere, or maybe even in many places, you're going to be reading about prayer. Today we like to read about prayer. We like to talk about prayer. We like to learn about prayer. What is our challenge, then? We don't get around to actually praying nearly enough. Too often our lives are filled with the noise of twenty-first century life: the television, the computer, the radio, the I-pod, or else just the "noise" of everyday living. We are a distracted people. And this has separated us more from God than anything else ever has before. It is time that all of us take an honest, serious look at our prayer lives. St. Francis has much to say to us about this.

St. Francis of Assisi would be amazed at us. He wouldn't understand how and why we profess to follow Jesus and say that we love Him, but then turn around and fail to spend any real quality time with Him on a regular basis. He would remind us that this would never fly in any of our other relationships. Just try going weeks without talking with your spouse, or your parents, or your children, or your boss, or your best friend, and then just see the damage that a lack of communication can do to ANY relationship, including our relationship with God. St. Francis, St. Clare, all of their early followers, and all of the saints of the Catholic Church recognized this fact: you are not going to get any closer to God if you are NOT praying.

One of my favorite examples of both St. Francis's faith and his trust in prayer comes from the later days of his life. According to the *Actus*, St Francis was on his way Rieti to go see a doctor for his eyes at the urging of Cardinal Hugolin. This would have been in 1224 or 1225. As they neared the city, a great crowd came out to see the saint. With St. Francis suffering greatly with his eyes, and trying to avoid the large number of people wanting to see him, the little group of Franciscans stopped at a local church to rest for the final leg of the journey. The crowd, however, found out that they were there, and the little church and its surrounding property were overwhelmed with all kinds of people. St. Francis ended up staying there for several days because he saw the great good that God was doing among the people. People were returning to their faith, they were going to confession, and they were being filled with the love of God. Much good was being accomplished. Handling the crowds, though, was not easy. In fact, the local priest had a small vineyard on the church property that had been all but destroyed and trampled underfoot by the great crowd. The priest didn't say anything, but internally he wished that he had not allowed St. Francis to stay at his church. St. Francis knew his thoughts, and he asked the priest how many measures of wine his vineyard produced each year. The priest answered, "Twelve." St. Francis then asked the priest to let him stay on at his church and to be patient with the crowds, as they continued to convert their hearts. St. Francis even went so far to promise the priest that if he would cooperate, God would bless him with twenty measures of wine that year. The priest put his trust in what St. Francis had promised. St Francis and the crowds stayed on there for several more days. By the end of the visit, the vineyard was nearly destroyed and only a few bunches of grapes were left on the trampled vines. But when vintage time came, the priest trusting in the saint's promise, gathered those little bunches of grapes, put them into the wine press, and pressed them. And just as St. Francis had promised, twenty measures of the very best wine were obtained from those very few bunches of grapes! There was no doubt for the priest and the people of that area that St. Francis's prayers and intercession had brought about the miracle. St. Francis had a compete trust that God would take care of the situation. And that is exactly the way that he prayed and interceded. Isn't it also the way that we should pray?

Prayer, any of the thousands of types of prayer, keeps us connected to God. Prayer is not so much for God. God doesn't need our prayers. And yet God certainly enjoys our turning to Him at all the different times of our lives, and acknowledging His power and authority. Prayer is for us. It gives us a larger perspective in the good times and the bad times of our lives. It can give us a whole new perspective on everything! Prayer changes us. Prayer keeps us plugged into God's love and grace, the power source of the Christian life, and it tethers us to God during the craziest and stormiest times of our lives.

We know that prayer was always so very important to St. Francis. From the earliest days of his conversion on the outskirts of Assisi to his death at Santa Maria degli Angeli on Oct. 3rd, 1226, St. Francis was talking AND listening to God. The Liturgy of the Hours was a main staple of St. Francis's life and the Franciscan Order. The Friars would always stop whatever they were doing when it was time for prayer. The Holy Mass and praying before the Holy Eucharist were also essential elements of Franciscan life.

And St. Francis prayed about everything. The story of the priest's vineyard proves that. There was nothing that was too small or unimportant that it shouldn't be taken to God. What an important message for all of us! How many times do we think that we don't need to "bother" God with so many different aspects of our lives, when what God most desires is EVERY aspect of our lives, the good and the bad, to be brought to Him! Do we only tell our spouse or our best friend part of what's going on in our lives? No, we don't. Why in the world would we attempt that with God?

What is our biggest obstacle to prayer? It is our time. We think that we don't have enough time to have a good prayer life. And you know what? If we're constantly on the computer, or in front of the TV, or even working on good and holy projects, we're not going to have time for real prayer. We're going to wonder why we feel "disconnected". We need to set aside time. I would even add to this we need to set aside a particular space to pray. Eighty percent of our challenges with prayer could be taken care of if we simply found the best time of the day for us to pray, and then set that time aside ONLY for prayer. And if we would just do the same thing with a place to pray, we would see that the right place for praying can make all the difference. You can't pray with distractions or constant interruption. It won't work. I promise you: you find the right time and the right place, and you already have the hardest part of making your prayer life better taken care of. And it will only get better from there.

In the musical *Fiddler On The Roof*, the main character, Tevye, spends the entire play talking to God. For Tevye, there is no time or situation that is off limits for talking to God. In good times and in bad, when he is at work and when he is resting, when he is with others and when he is alone, when he is happy and when he is sad, when he is hope-filled and when he is full of desperation, Tevye is praying to God. Prayer for this devout Jewish man is an on-going dialogue with God our Father. What a beautiful example for all of us to follow! So many times we think that we can only pray when we are happy, or when things are going our way, or only when we are in church, or even only when we feel like talking to God. None of that is true. God wants us in communication with Him all day, all week, all year, all of our lives! How much better we could all be if only we prayed in that same way.

St. Francis of Assisi gives us a real life example of Tevye's kind of faith. Prayer was constant and on-going for St. Francis; he wasn't afraid to set aside time and space. It didn't bother him at all to tell people that he needed time alone with God, and people respected him and his request. My fear is that we, as people of faith today, are afraid to set those kind of boundaries and draw those kind of lines. We think that we need to be constantly available and always on call; that is especially true for those of us who work in the Church today. Jesus Himself wasn't constantly available! Remember Martha reminding Jesus that He wasn't there when Lazarus died? Sometimes we're not going to be there, as much as we want to be, and that's alright. Jesus also wasn't afraid to retreat to spend time with His Father, and He certainly thought it was important for His first disciples to go and do the same thing, most importantly before or after work was done. St. Francis also bought into this part of the Gospel whole-heartedly. The work was important but the work wasn't going to get done at all without faith and prayer. We, however, run on and on without "filling up" our spiritual tanks and then we wonder why we feel like we're "running on empty"?

We can never do this thing called "Christianity" on our own. It will never work. It's not supposed to work that way. Prayer is our connection to our God and His love and His grace. He is the Vine and we are the branches, and prayer keeps us connected to that Vine. What is more important than that? What possible excuse can we make to God for not praying? That was St. Francis's perspective. St. Francis would weep when he saw a crucifix. He was moved to near ecstasy when he came into the presence of a nativity scene. Even walking by a church is said to have made the saint feel closer to God, Whom he felt was with him every minute of every day. What would it take for us to love Jesus that much in our lives? How different would our lives be if we recognized God's presence with us as much as St. Francis did? How could we NOT pray then?

And St. Francis didn't always have to be talking. Long hours of St. Francis's prayer were spent in listening to and waiting on God. Listening is such an important part of prayer! We forget this. We can't talk all the time. And there really is something to the fact that the saints have had great patience in prayer. They don't give up when they don't hear God right away, but they patiently wait for what God has in store for them. Too often if we don't see immediate results or get the answer that we want right away, we quit praying. It doesn't work that way. St. Francis teaches us patience in our prayer. We, like St. Francis, may even misunderstand what God is trying to tell us. That's alright. God will always get His message across to those who are truly trying to listen. St. Francis found that out so many times in his life. What God was doing with *Il Poverino* was so much bigger than St. Francis ever imagined. All he had to do was keep listening. And so must we!

Give God the chance. Talk to Him from your heart. Listen to Him with your soul. And continue to find new and better ways to pray. There are no "right" ways and "wrong" ways; there's only prayer! Staying connected to Jesus makes it all worth it. It is how all of us can become saints!

"THOSE WHO HAVE GOD ARE SHORT OF NOTHING. GOD ALONE IS ENOUGH."

(St. Teresa of Avila

"But when you pray, go to your inner room, close the door, and pray to your Father in secret. And your Father who sees in secret will repay you."

Matthew 6:6

"MESSAGES FROM ASSISI" - DISCUSSION
GUIDELINE QUESTIONS

Chapter #12 - Prayer

A. Your best experience of prayer is… what? What made it so good?

B. Your worst experience of prayer is… what made it so bad? What did you learn from it?

C. Who in your life has taught you to pray? Who has been your best example of a "person of prayer"?

D. What aspects of St. Francis' prayer life most make sense to you? What does St. Francis most teach us about prayer?

E. How have you seen your prayer life grow over the years? What has helped it most? What has hindered it most?

F. What do you most want to pass on to your children and grandchildren about prayer?

CHAPTER THIRTEEN
Francis And Clare: A Holy Friendship

"When you go about the world do not quarrel or fight with words, or judge others; rather, be meek, peaceful and unassuming, gentle and humble, speaking courteously to everyone as is becoming."

St. Francis of Assisi

Perhaps the single most over-exposed area of the life of St. Francis at the beginning of the 21st Century is his relationship with St. Clare of Assisi. Inquiring minds want to know, as the old ads for *The National Inquirer* used to say. The relationship between two of the Catholic Church's greatest saints who were both contemporaries AND from the same small town in Italy, is perfect fodder for juicy speculation and historic conjecture. And yet, perhaps no other area of the life of St. Francis is as important to our understanding of his spirituality and what he has to teach us today, as his friendship with St. Clare.

St. Francis of Assisi was twelve years older than St. Clare. Assisi is not that big of a town, not now and not then, so it seems likely that the two saints must have known each other on some level. Perhaps St. Clare went with her mother to St. Francis's father's store to buy fine cloth for their home and clothes. St. Francis may have noticed the cute little girl with her family across the aisle at Mass on Sunday at San Ruffino where both of them were baptized. We don't know exactly when or where that they met, despite their age difference, but by the time of Francis's conversion, it is clear that each was aware of the other. Their relationship was unique, and appreciating that relationship is vitally important to understanding the lives of both saints.

In 1194 Clare was born into one of Assisi's richest and most powerful families. Her father was Count Favarone di Offreduccio and her mother was Donna Ortolana, of the Fiumi family, both of noble heritage, tracing their ancestry back to the time of Charlemagne. Clare was born and lived with her family in a splendid palace at Piazza San Ruffino. It would have been one of most beautiful and most protected homes in Assisi. They lived on the same square where Assisi's cathedral was built. Clare had two younger sisters, Catherine and Beatrice. According to St. Clare's canonization documents, as a teenager Clare was very beautiful with "an oval face, her forehead spacious, her color dazzling, and her eyebrows and hair very fair." The documents continue to describe her with "a celestial smile that played in her eyes and round her mouth." With beauty, money, power, a good family, and lots of friends, certainly Clare would have seemed to have it all. And yet, from very early on in her life, Clare also had a very compassionate and generous aspect to her personality. Even as a child, Clare was giving food and other necessities to the poor and to those less fortunate. Clare's mother was a pious woman and deeply involved in her faith, making pilgrimages to Rome and even the Holy Land, and making it a priority to pass on her Christianity to her daughters. Living right next door to the Cathedral of Assisi probably made it hard to avoid faith and the Church. Clare was the antithesis to St. Francis's party-boy image of growing up in Assisi at that time. Clare spurned many suitors who asked her parents for her hand in marriage because she always wanted more; she came to believe that only God could truly make her happy. St. Francis would come to this same conclusion, but it would take him much longer.

When Clare came to the season of Lent in 1212, as a seventeen year-old girl, she heard St. Francis preach a series of homilies in both San Giorgio, where the current Basilica of St. Clare is located, and San Ruffino. The homilies changed her life. St. Francis's words were giving a voice and an understanding to exactly what Clare had been feeling and experiencing for years. Clare was enthralled. Someone else understood. Someone else knew and loved God the way that she did.

Clare firmly believed that God had sent St. Francis to her to let her know what she was supposed to do next in her conversion. The relationship was not typical of the physical, the material, and the mutually-exclusive companionship that marks so many of our relationships today. By this time in their lives, both were too far in love with God to get distracted by each other. But what they became was the perfect help to each other's vocation and faith, and that allowed both of them to become saints. So much so that today it becomes impossible to imagine St. Clare without St. Francis, and vice-versa, St. Francis of Assisi without St. Clare. There's no juicy story here, but there is a love story; it is a triangle involving all three: St. Francis, St. Clare, and Jesus Christ. Without the common denominator of Jesus Christ, would St. Francis and St. Clare have loved each other? It is doubtful.

St. Francis and St. Clare have a great deal to teach all of us today about friendship and love. It is so important for us as Christians, again even more importantly for us as Catholic Christians, to have strong friendships in Christ. Living the Christian life and following the Christian way is so much easier when we have people to share the journey with and who understand the Christian spiritual life. I would even go so far to say that today you're not going to make it very far in the Christian life WITHOUT some really good Christian friends around you. This is even true of marriage and marital love. We all need others who help us to be better, to help us to hear and understand what God is trying to tell us, and to help us to realize that we are not alone or crazy in our relationships with God. St. Francis and St. Clare found that in each other. They were enthralled every time they were blessed with the opportunity to talk or to visit with each other, or even when they received messages from each other. This was not because the other person excited them. It was because the other person helped them to see and experience God that much better in their own life, and every encounter, every word, even every mention of the other's name, reminded them both of just how real God is and what that very real God was doing in both of their lives.

St. Francis would go home to the Lord in October 3rd of 1226, at the age of 44. St. Clare would go on to live a relatively long life, joining St. Francis in that Kingdom that they both longed for at the age of 60, on August 11th, 1253. For two and half decades, much longer than she was friends with him, Clare had to carry on the dream that they both shared alone. She became one of the ardent defenders of the Franciscan way of life, when even many of St. Francis's own brothers would lose their way. Uncompromisingly, she stood up to the Pope and many others who wanted her to "water-down" her way of life for her sisters and separate them from the Franciscan family. St. Clare's perseverance in Christ and in the Franciscan way of life, especially after St. Francis's death, is certainly a role model for all of us. We all need such friends. And we need to all remain loyal and faithful to such friends, even after death separates us, if only for a little while.

Also like St. Francis's father, St. Clare's father had little understanding for the choices that his eldest daughter was making and her conversion. Today we romanticize about Clare's Palm Sunday night escape from their palace and getting out of Assisi's venerable walls at night and her flight to Saint Mary of the Angels. But the reality is that it took even more courage for St. Clare to leave home and join St. Francis than it did for St. Francis himself to do it. What Clare did was unheard of for a girl of noble birth. Clare's family had big plans for her. The day after her night escape, Clare's father was livid. He sent his armed troops, led by his powerful brother, Monaldo, to retrieve his daughter. But Clare's absolute resolution to stay, literally clinging to the altar and the altar clothes, eventually sent the little army back to Assisi. Two months later, things would go very differently when St. Clare's younger sister, Catherine, who was given the religious name "Agnes", would follow in her big sister's footsteps, and also leave the palace to join the order that would bear her sister's name. This time, Uncle Monaldo and his men were not so easily dissuaded and young Catherine was nearly beaten to death by her uncle in trying to force her to return home. Eventually St. Clare's family story ends much better than St. Francis's, with both of her sisters and her mother, the Countess Ortolana, joining St. Clare at the convent at San Damiano in the Poor Clares. With St. Francis, we have no records or indicators that he saw either Pietro or Pica ever again, following the episode at the Bishop's residence where he gave his father his clothes back and renounced his sonship. It might seem harsh to us today, but both St. Francis and St. Clare had to leave their families, especially in both cases their fathers, to become what God wanted them to be. Perhaps this also was part of their common bond; they became family for each other.

St. Francis of Assisi and St. Clare BOTH changed the Church forever back in the thirteenth century. Their friendship and shared faith enabled both of them to be better followers of Christ. How many friends do we have who do that for us? For how many of our friends do we make that same commitment to their ongoing conversion? We're supposed to be in this "building-the-Kingdom-of-God thing" together. We need each other; we need to be true friends to each other. In modern times the whole notion of friendship has been so radically cheapened and prostituted. People are friends today on Facebook and Skype solely based on the fact that we have given others information about ourselves. Isn't true friendship much more than that? Isn't it time that all of us came to expect more from our friendships, and that we more clearly defined who our true friends really are? Which of your friends are helping you to become a saint?

The relationship of St. Francis of Assisi and St. Clare was an extraordinary friendship. They became inspiration to each other to hear what God was saying and then to find the courage to do what God asked. How extremely important it is that we learn to do that for one another. May we, too, strive to have many holy friendships. May we seek friends and even acquaintances who will help us to be better and to be more of what Christ intended us to be. Many times those kinds of friendships come from unexpected places. We must remember that St. Francis of Assisi never would have imagined as a young man that his life would have been so affected by a young girl, so much younger than he was. Sometimes God uses very surprising people to get us where we need to be. And sometimes those people who God sends to us become some of our best friends. Pay close attention to the people that God sends to you. You never know. One of them, or many of them, may be exactly who you need to become a saint!

"Some friends bring ruin on us, but a true friend is more loyal than a brother."

Proverbs 18:24

"MESSAGES FROM ASSISI" – DISCUSSION GUIDELINE QUESTIONS

Chapter #13 - Francis and Clare: a Holy Friendship

A. What makes a friendship "holy"? How is it different? How do you make or keep a relationship holy? Is it important for us to have holy relationships? Why or why not?

B. Think for a moment of the people in your life who support you in your faith…what characterizes your relationship with them? How do they help you? How do you help them?

C. What are the most difficult parts of working together as brothers and sisters in the Church? Why isn't it easier? What can we do to better work together in the building up of the Kingdom of God?

D. How has God surprised you with the people that he has brought into your life? Has God ever used someone that you would least expect, to draw you closer to himself and lead you to greater holiness? Why, perhaps, after you got to know the person who was the surprise, maybe it wasn't so surprising after all?

CHAPTER FOURTEEN

On Fighting Sin And Temptation

"That person sins who wishes to receive more from his neighbor than what he is willing to give of himself to the Lord God."

St. Francis of Assisi

When dealing with any of the saints of the Church, it's very easy for us to think of them as somehow beyond us, very different from us, and removed from the ordinary that all of us who are still alive face every single day. It is hard for us to imagine St. Catherine of Siena exhausted from a hard day's work, or St. Charles Borromeo frustrated by his co-workers, or even closer to our own time, St. Pio of Pietracina or St. Teresa of Calcutta truly at the end of their patience because of what people around them expected of them. And yet, the Church holds up the saints for us to imitate and follow precisely because they were very human, human beings.

Let's be very clear about this: the saints were not perfect. All of them dealt with sin, temptation, frustrations, and weakness. From the very beginning, with the Apostles—the very foundation of our Church—the very best faltered. They denied Christ; they were weak; many times they were unable to do what God asked of them. The saints have much to teach us about sinfulness and temptation. They all were tempted. At some point and in some way, all of them fell and sinned. They all went to Confession. They have all been where we have been, and with God's help they triumphed. Once again I would say that quite possibly there is no better example of this than St. Francis of Assisi.

Throughout his life St. Francis was acutely aware of his sinfulness and weakness. He did harsh penances for his own sins and for the sins of the world. St. Francis knew well about pride, greed, lust, gluttony, sloth, and jealousy. He knew about these sins and temptations, not because he read about them in a book or someone told him about them, but because he had personally experienced battles within himself between what God wanted and the lies with which the devil sought to lure St. Francis. St. Francis battled these things from the very earliest days of his conversion, right up until the day that he died, lying on the ground at St. Mary of the Angels. We cannot spend this time with St. Francis and his teachings without recognizing that Il Poverino is exactly who we can look to in order to find out how to battle sin and temptation in our lives.

The first thing that St. Francis teaches us is that in our relationship with God we must develop a real humility. God is leading us to holiness, not the other way around. We are never going to make ourselves holy. This is so hard for us to accept! We want to do it, but it just doesn't work that way. We can only trust and cooperate with God and His Holy Will.

St. Francis learned this first lesson early on in his conversion. He was continually misunderstanding God, even as the Cross of San Damiano spoke to him. Rebuilding the stone walls of San Damiano was and is a noble cause, but it was not what God intended for St. Francis to do with his life. God Himself would correct the misunderstanding and get St. Francis to where He wanted him to be. St. Francis reminds all of us that this same God greatly desires to do the same thing for all of us, and all we have to do is to be listening humbly. We have to be willing to give God's way and His commandments a chance to work in our lives. God will always prove himself. But that is never going to happen if we fail to give Him the opportunity to show us that His way is better. Sometimes this very much means that we have to admit that we are/were wrong, and go back and start over again, just as St. Francis did. True discernment of what God wants of us demands that we not be afraid to turn back to listen all over again. It takes a lot of humility, and it takes a good deal of patience with ourselves and with God.

To effectively battle sin and temptation we also need to have a bigger picture of what is going on. St. Francis, as were most of the saints, was graced with a much bigger vision of things than just what this world offers. To see from an eternal perspective, to whole-heartedly value the Kingdom of Heaven that we have been promised, and to live our lives so that absolutely nothing gets in the way of our participation in that Kingdom, changes everything for us as sinners. Suddenly there is new reason for us to follow God's commands and to live lives of holiness. We need that perspective and that new rationale in our lives today. We have great incentive to keep fighting sin and temptation. Heaven is in the balance here! We don't want to ever forget how important it is for us to live our lives the right way—Jesus's way. St. Francis had such an awareness of this. He was so committed to listening well and doing the right thing!

St. Francis was also acutely aware that we are in the middle of a great battle between God and Satan. There is much that we don't know about this. But what we do know is that both God and Satan greatly desire our souls, which are the very essence of who we really are. St. Francis knew all too well the reality of this battle. He had such a powerful revelation of what God had done through the incarnation and the Cross to save our souls; God's love and desire for our souls was so evident to him. And yet St. Francis also knew firsthand the desperate measures that Satan will take, the perfect lies that he will tell, to get us to fall and to join his side. Deception, the perversion of the truth, is what the devil is all about. There's a reason why Jesus refers to the devil as "the father of lies" in the Sacred Scriptures. All of our great sins are perversions of the truth. St. Francis knew that if the devil can get us to believe any of his lies, we are in trouble. This is why God's truth and the power of God's way were the priorities that St. Francis came to live by.

One of the lesser known stories from *The Little Flowers* is the story of how St. Francis helped Brother Rufino beat a temptation of the devil. It seems that Brother Rufino, one of the early companions of St.

Francis and a man of great holiness, was greatly tempted concerning predestination. Satan even appeared to Brother Rufino in the image of the Crucified Christ telling him that he and St. Francis were damned, and that he should not believe. Brother Rufino was extremely upset by this vision, and the lies he was told began to affect his outlook and his faith. God made St. Francis aware of this turmoil. So St. Francis sent for him, concerned that Brother Rufino believed the lies of the devil without coming to him seeking help and spiritual guidance. At first reluctant, but then realizing that he had been deceived, Brother Rufino went to St. Francis and sought his advice. St. Francis told Brother Rufino that the next time the devil tells him that he is damned, "You answer him confidently, 'Open your mouth – and I will [empty my bowels] in it.'" *The Little Flowers* cleans this up quite a bit, but you get the point. St. Francis, one of the greatest saints of the Catholic Church, is telling his friend and follower, Brother Rufino, to deal with the devil on his own terms and in his own language. St. Francis promises Brother Rufino that at those words the devil will immediately go away and that this should be a sign that it is the devil. St. Francis also pointed out that another sign that it was the devil and not God speaking, was that the demon had hardened Brother Rufino's heart to all that was good, cutting him off from all that was of lasting value. If we are really honest, isn't this still one of Satan's favorite tricks when it comes to our sins and our temptations?

St. Francis's advice to Brother Rufino is really excellent advice for all of us for all ages. We are too nice when it comes to our dealings with the devil. We don't take a stand. We give him too much of a chance for success when we are not clearly against sin and temptation. If ever there was a time for vulgarity and for being definitive in our stand against evil, it is when we are tempted most clearly by the devil himself. "Open your mouth and I will [empty my bowels] down your throat" is pretty definitive! No other story from *The Little Flowers* was more surprising to me than this one.

But you see the point, don't you? We must take a stand against sin in our lives. If we don't, we will keep falling over and over again until the sin becomes habitual. And if sin becomes habitual, then it is that much harder to root out of our lives. As twenty-first century

Christians we have played around with sin and temptation way too much. We have justified and rationalized the devil's lies to ourselves so that we like to pretend that sin isn't sin anymore. We don't kill babies anymore; we terminate pregnancies and get rid of "tissue". We don't live in sin anymore; we "cohabitate" and live "alternative lifestyles". We don't lie anymore, but we "embellish" the truth, or "stretch" it, or "shift our paradigms". We can't fight back if we're not honest with ourselves, with God, and even with the devil. St. Francis knew that. That's what he was trying to help Brother Rufino see!

We can beat the devil. Jesus is so much more powerful than Satan; St. Francis experienced that power and authority in a very real way in his own life. We too can conquer our sins. We can stand up to temptation. We just can't do it by ourselves. We need God's help. And we need God's help constantly!

We need the example of the saints. And we need to learn some new tricks in our fight against the devil. Too often we try to be good and do the right thing, and then we get tempted, and we fall to our temptations because we do things exactly the same way as we always have. To truly fight sin, we've got to change our usual responses. We've got to change the situation. We keep doing the same things the same old way, and seem surprised when we end up getting the same results. It shouldn't be a surprise.

Change the pattern and many times we can change our falling into sin. For St. Francis, everything was about the battle for holiness. St. Francis fasted from food and many other things. He offered up all kinds of bodily comforts. He pushed, and some would even say tortured, his body to keep it focused on God. There are stories of his rolling around in the snow or even rolling in the thorns of rose bushes at St. Mary of the Angels, to conquer the passions of his body. To us in modern times, these seem like such excesses, and yet these acts of penance truly worked for St. Francis and apparently also for his early brothers. I believe that the important thing is that St. Francis did SOMETHING to PREVENT his passions or appetites from controlling what he was doing. Too often today we do nothing, and then we wonder why we fall and why we fail. We must fight back; we must become fighters for the holiness of our souls. We must be willing to do whatever it takes to stay on track, on course, with Jesus Christ. Our choices matter. St. Francis made many of the right choices in his life, and so must we! Holiness is a great thing, but it is not just going "to happen" to us. We have to become better at making the right choices. We have to make some changes.

Of course, many times our sins are sins of omission. Not only do we need to be avoiding all occasions of sin, but we also need to be constantly looking for opportunities to do the right thing. In this area St. Francis also excelled. St. Francis saw every moment, every encounter, as an opportunity for doing good, for bringing God's love into the world, and for helping others. We would obviously not miss these opportunities if we were paying better attention to what's going on around us, and if we, through prayer, were better tuned into all of those incredible chances every day to bear witness to Christ and to spread His love. St. Francis of Assisi lived his life to not miss any of those opportunities on any given day. Can you imagine what we could do if we lived that way? Sins of omission happen so often just because we aren't paying attention to what we are supposed to be doing. We could change the world if we just paid better attention.

St. Francis was holy, and joyful, and filled with a great love of creation. But St. Francis never quit fighting sin and temptation in his life. He knew too well the dangers to his soul and the everlasting damage to his place in the Kingdom if he did. Too often we want to emphasize the first point, and avoid the second one here. And there is no way that we can see and understand the complete St. Francis, or his spirituality, without both perspectives.

"Watch carefully then how you live, not as foolish persons, but as wise, making the most of the opportunity, because the days are evil."

Ephesians 5: 15- 16

"MESSAGES FROM ASSISI" - DISCUSSION GUIDELINE QUESTIONS

Chapter #14 - On Fighting Sin and Temptation

A. The vast majority of saints, who knew their own sins well, never would have considered themselves "saints". And yet their faults and weaknesses also never became excuses to "give in" to sinfulness. How can we learn that kind of perseverance?

B. "Avoiding the occasions of sin" is more than just a nice saying that the nuns used to tell us. If we are serious about rooting sin out of our lives, it is what we must do. Why are we so reluctant to make the necessary changes to really live holy lives? Where can we get the strength and courage to make changes?

C. How do we keep our eyes, our hearts, and our lives set on heaven, while we are living in this world? In the middle of "everybody" else living for today and this world, how do we as catholic Christians keep heaven as our highest goal and stay committed to it?

D. Why are we so afraid to acknowledge the spiritual warfare that goes on around us every day? How is our pretending it doesn't exist causing us to lose the battle before it starts?

CHAPTER FIFTEEN

Discovering A New Side Of Christ — Greccio And The Crib

"Above all the graces and gifts of the Holy Spirit is that of conquering oneself and willingly enduring sufferings, insults, humiliations and hardships for the love of Christ... If we endure cruel rebuffs patiently, without being troubled and without complaining, and if we reflect humbly and charitably when others speak against us - perfect joy is there!

St. Francis of Assisi

I suppose that it was only a matter of time for the man and the saint who had such a strong attraction and devotion to the Cross and the Crucified Christ, to discover a similar kind of love for Jesus from the beginning of His life with the Nativity. For St. Francis this happened at Greccio, Italy, a remote mountain-top village about two hours south of Assisi. It was the Christmas of 1223, and St. Francis was in Greccio to pray and find some peace following the dismantling of his second Rule. This was not a happy time in the saint's life. He was tired and hurt, and he felt betrayed by the order that he himself had founded and that bore his name. He certainly must have felt that all of his work up to this point in his life had been undone by the watered-down and compromised version of the new Rule for the Franciscan Order. Taking along just a few of his most trusted brothers, who also must have felt that the order, the Franciscan family that they loved and to which they had committed their lives, was betraying them, St. Francis went to a hermitage at Greccio that was on the property of a friend. At that time, the hermitage was pretty much nothing more than a cave in the side of the mountain. Today, the hermitage at Greccio is a beautiful and inspiring sanctuary that is one of the favorite places of St. Francis's devotees to visit. While in prayer at Greccio, in the midst of all the turmoil that was going on in his life at the time, St. Francis fell in love with the Infant Jesus. Remember, it had always been the Crucified Christ that had been at the heart of St. Francis's spirituality. St. Francis reasoned that the Incarnation had to happen before we could get to the Cross. At Greccio, St. Francis became even more aware of what an extraordinary gift God had given us in the simple act of coming down into the world.

Completely mesmerized by this new insight, St. Francis of Assisi went to his friend who owned the property and asked his permission and his assistance in organizing a Christmas pageant that would take place on a beautiful, wooded plain down just below the hermitage, immediately before Midnight Mass. It would be a living pageant, with real animals and living people playing the various roles of the Nativity story from the Gospel. This spectacle would share St. Francis' new-found love of the Nativity of the Christ with everyone. It would bring many others into the story, both those who would be asked to perform the various roles, and all of the people from the local countryside who were going to be invited to come and share Christmas Eve with the Franciscans.

With his friend's help, they brought together the entire village and went to work on what would become the world's first nativity scene. Elaborate sets, live animals, candles and torches, and the town folk who played various roles recreated the scene from Bethlehem that Christmas right there on a small plain at Greccio. All in attendance were deeply moved by St. Francis's creation. The nativity story did indeed come to life for each of them. St. Francis stood next to the Nativity scene and preached a Christmas homily that was filled with emotion, love, and commitment. He brought the birth of a poor Messiah to life for those attending. This Messiah was born not on silk sheets, but on the hay and straw in a barn. St. Francis's great love was even more evident than his superb words and speaking abilities. The people there that Christmas Eve were mesmerized! They got it, and they left changed by the love of God. St. Francis had started a tradition that not only the Franciscan Order, but indeed, all Christians carry on today.

My brothers and sisters, this story is very important for several reasons. First, we get a very real glimpse of the saint still getting to know Christ even more. St. Francis was so close to Jesus! Perhaps he was closer to our Lord than any person or any saint since Mary and the Apostles. He had an intimacy with God that so many of us would come to envy and seek to find in our own lives. And yet at Greccio, while at prayer in a cave of all places, Il Poverino got to know our Lord in an even deeper way.

How important this is for all of us! We are never done getting to know Jesus. None of us are. He is always new. Jesus is always revealing more of Himself to us. Christmas, of course, is the perfect time to remember this, but shouldn't we really remember this all year around? Sometimes we can get so comfortable, so secure in our faith and our relationships with Jesus that we fail to let Him show us more. St. Francis's experience at Greccio is a challenge to all of us to make sure that we are letting Jesus continue to reveal Himself to us, even in new and different ways—sometimes even in ways that we would never expect or anticipate. Sometimes Jesus reminds all of us that we have a very surprising God. He doesn't want anybody getting bored or complacent.

Secondly, we see in St. Francis a newfound joy and enthusiasm for evangelization. The saint still wants to share the Good News with others. And remember, this is just three years before his death. St. Francis is in his early forties and has many health issues. This is not exactly when we would be expecting someone to re-define and rediscover his spiritual life. And yet St. Francis goes right back to his primary mission of preaching the Gospel. And now he is going to tell the nativity story of Jesus, involving hundreds of other people, and as a production that will allow even more hundreds to experience it. And the Gospel gets passed on.

The Gospel is a real, living thing, and St. Francis is making it even more intelligible for everyone—the young and the old, the rich and the poor, the literate and the illiterate. And St. Francis loved doing this. This is so important for us all to realize. Nothing brought St. Francis more joy than sharing Jesus and God with others! Nothing! This is the disease of all of those who preach. St. Francis rediscovers his life and his spirit at Greccio because he got back to preaching. The saint, just like St. Paul, was compelled to preach the Gospel. This story is for us all. We hear this story, and we all become a part of it. It gets passed on to us. And then guess what? Then, we too become preachers of the story, the Gospel, and then it gets handed on to others by us! And even more importantly, the story, the Gospel, is a part of all of us! It resonates in our lives. We must preach it; we must live it; sometimes we must use words. And sometimes, maybe, we must use a nativity set. We just can't truly hear the Word of God and not preach it.

Finally, and maybe most powerfully, we see the saint, at what quite possibly was one of the lowest points in his life, find new joy and rejuvenation in the same place where he originally found it so many years earlier in front of the Cross of San Damiano—with Jesus! I really want for us to ponder this for a while. Certainly St. Francis of Assisi still felt the "sting" of what he must have considered a betrayal of some of his closest followers in the Franciscan Order and also the betrayal of the Pope in Rome who had backed the "less strict" version of the new Rule. In many ways St. Francis came to Greccio a broken soul. And yet, St. Francis's sadness and disappointment are turned around by a Christ Who won't be watered-down, or "revised" or made to be something that He is not. St. Francis found a certain confirmation for himself in the Nativity story, that the poor Christ child, born in a manger with nothing, was backing St. Francis's views on poverty. And with that confirmation and support, St. Francis knew that nothing else really mattered. At Greccio, St. Francis found healing and forgiveness for all the hurt and disappointment that he had experienced in the mess of the writing and approval of the New Rule. He found a new joy in his work, in his mission, and in his life.

What an incredible lesson for all of us when we feel beat up, disillusioned, betrayed, or let down! And again, from the last chapter, those feelings are so much more intense when it comes to our faith, our relationship with God, and with the Church. We all know what this is like! And if you don't understand what I am talking about right now, then you haven't been really involved in the Church long enough yet, because I promise you that if you stay really involved, you will! It happens to all of us. When you think about it, it even happened to Jesus! Who was the very first person betrayed by the Church? Wasn't it Christ Himself? Like Jesus, and like St. Francis of Assisi, we need to learn to forgive and move on, and to get back to work proclaiming the Gospel. This is because the proclamation of the Gospel is what's most important. The story is bigger than all of us; in the end, nobody is going to stop the Gospel. We have messed it up; we have gotten it wrong; we have fallen away from it. But in the end, we are always called back to the Truth, and the Truth is what always lasts.

If you are reading these words right now and you have been hurt by the Church, or more likely individuals within the Church, by their thoughts, words, or actions, I am sorry for your hurt. As a member of the Church, and even more as a leader within the Church, I am humbly reminded many times every day of just how far we still have yet to go in our own conversion. The Church, and any of its parts or members, is not perfect. We never have been in our past, and we certainly are not so today. But we always have hope for the future. Jesus called us to be "perfect as our Heavenly Father is perfect". And clearly we have a long way to go. And yet our own hurt, anger, disappointment, disillusionment, or even betrayal can't keep us away. The Church needs each one of us too badly for us to allow that to happen. And honestly, each of us, too, needs the Church much, much more than we know most of the time.

It is interesting that so many of the saints, not just St. Francis of Assisi, suffered such intense trials with the very Church that they loved and were committed to being a part of. The terrible persecutions that Padre Pio would endure as a Franciscan, even seven hundred years after the time of St. Francis, remind us that we really haven't come that far. It is somehow expected that as Christians we are going to face trials and tribulations from Satan and from the world; in fact the Sacred Scriptures even promise us that. It just seems so much harder to handle when some of the most difficult and most trying challenges come from within the Church itself. Jealously, pride, and selfishness have wreaked havoc on the Church over the centuries. And yet, if you notice, St. Francis of Assisi, Padre Pio, and ALL of the saints persevered in their Catholic faith. They trusted that God had a plan even when they couldn't see it or understand it, and none of them, despite their trials at the hand of the Church, left it or went anywhere else. Even during the worst of days with the Franciscan Order, and with bishops and even the Pope supporting those who St. Francis firmly believed were destroying what he had spent his life building up, at no point does St. Francis ever consider leaving the order or the Church. And what does that say? Let us not only acknowledge that witness that he gave us, but let us also allow that witness to inspire us the next time that we get upset at something or someone in the Church today. That's the kind of real faith and real trust that I want to have more of in my life.

We all need more healing and forgiveness in our lives! St. Francis found it at Greccio. I wonder, when and where are you going to allow God to bring healing and peace to your life? What would you have to do to forgive those who have hurt you or persecuted you? Do you need to go on a retreat or a pilgrimage? Do you need an hour of Adoration? Do you need to spend more time reading the Sacred Scriptures? Or can reading a book about St. Francis allow the healing to start in your soul? With Christ, all things are possible! There are millions of ways for us to come to peace. Sometimes each and every one of us needs God's joy to return to our lives. May we do whatever we need to do to make that happen!

So the next time you see a Nativity scene, or manger, or crèche, or whatever else we may call it, say a prayer of thanksgiving to the saint from Assisi. Take a few extra moments to look at it and to be renewed in your faith. The joy of Christmas is not for just one day in December or even for a few days in December and January as the Church celebrates it. The real joy of Christmas is forever, no matter what is going on in our lives. And that's a message we all have to preach.

"For God so loved the world that He gave His only Son so that everyone who believes in Him might not perish but might have eternal life."

John 3:16

"MESSAGES FROM ASSISI" - DISCUSSION GUIDELINE QUESTIONS

Chapter #15 - The Second Rule of the Franciscan Order

A. Why is and why was living a vow of poverty such a radical thing, even for Franciscans? Why is it so hard for us to live in this world and not be of this world? Can you see how and why the debate over simplicity of life nearly tore the Franciscan order apart from the earliest of days?

B. As a Christian, how do you deal with disappointment and disillusionment in your faith life? Have you ever had an experience like St. Francis had, with the Church or with your brothers and sisters in the Church? What did you do about it? How did you "move on"? What can all of us do, to recover from past hurts and disappointments in our faith life?

C. Why is it so hard to be Church? What can we do together as a Church to make it easier for people to "get out of themselves" and to help them see a bigger picture?

D. How do we help our injured or even angry brothers and sisters to get back involved in the Church again?

CHAPTER SIXTEEN
The Second Rule Of The Franciscan Order

"He has sent you into the entire world for this reason: that in word and deed you may give witness to His voice and bring everyone to know that there is no one who is all-powerful except Him."

St. Francis of Assisi

By the year 1220, it became clear to everyone that a new Rule for the Franciscan was necessary. Perhaps the last person to be convinced of this was St. Francis himself. By this time, he had long before turned over the day-to-day governance of the order to others, who he hand-picked and trusted with the administration of the order. He never wanted the Franciscan Order to have a superior. All were to be brothers with the Holy Spirit guiding the lot of them. St. Francis himself strongly disdained the use of the term "Master" or "Superior". But St. Francis did strongly desire that all those who sought to follow him, keep the Gospel way of life to which he and the early followers had pledged their lives. In fact, the original Rule, hastily penned by St. Francis himself and taken by him and his original twelve friars to Pope Innocent III in Rome in 1209, was for the most part a collection of Gospel verses extolling poverty and evangelization. That Rule, that was given at least oral approval by the Pope, saw the order through the first decade. But because of the rapid growth of the Franciscan Order, more rules and more regulations were required to organize such a huge group. Literally, by 1219, thousands of men and women had come to join

St. Francis in his work. St. Francis still wanted the simplicity of the early days, but translating that simplicity to thousands of new members, especially when St. Francis was less and less involved in the day-to-day work of the order, became a great problem. With pressure from the leaders of his own community, several bishops that he trusted and relied on, and even from the papacy itself, in 1220 and 1221 St. Francis undertook to write a second Rule.

Of primary importance for St. Francis was that the poverty and simplicity of the order be maintained for all. The new Rule originally would argue for little change and that radical Gospel poverty would be at the heart of Franciscan life. St. Francis's new Rule consisted of twenty-four chapters of exhortations to love and follow Christ and to love each other. In it, St. Francis is clearly a father urging all of his children to love God and to get along. For St. Francis this was enough. Rules and regulations are not necessary for a person who has truly given their heart to the Lord. For St. Francis, the Franciscan life wasn't something you forced someone into, but rather something that they freely chose. To legislate the Franciscan life was to render it completely meaningless, for its Founder. The new Rule was not well-accepted.

Deep divisions arose among the supporters of St. Francis and those who had desired a more lenient version of the Rule. The joy of the saint and of the order was suddenly displaced by anxiety, anger, and division. St. Francis wrote: "I love the brothers with all my heart, but if they followed in my footsteps I should love them even more, I should not become a stranger in their midst." The divisions tore at the heart of the saint, perhaps more than any other suffering that he had previously endured. Something had to be done. In 1223 St. Francis took Brother Leo and Brother Bonizio with him to Fonte Columbo to pray and fast, and then start work on a new version. Shorter and more succinct than the Rule of 1221, St. Francis returned to the Portiuncula and hand-delivered the new Rule to Brother Elias, who was the new minister general of the order. Brother Elias, disappointed that the Founder didn't make enough changes to the Rule of 1221, conveniently "misplaced" the revised edition. St. Francis, without confronting Brother Elias or blaming him in any way, immediately headed back to Fonte Columbo and dictates the new Rule to Brother Leo for a second time. This is presented at the next general chapter meeting, where discussions lead to many changes being made. Finally, in a papal bill dated November 29th, 1223, Pope Honorus III endorses the Rule, which remains in effect today as the official Rule of the Franciscan Order.

- 2 -

The new Rule was a source of great sadness for the saint. St. Francis thought that men that he had at one time trusted, had watered-down and made meaningless his own words. The one tenet that St. Francis would not give up or compromise on was the absolute that no Franciscan should ever own a house, or land, or be involved in the exchange of money. St. Francis thought this the one uncompromising feature of the new Rule, which so little resembled his own work, would keep the Franciscan Order close to Lady Poverty.

I tell you this long tale, which I have so much abbreviated to give you just a basic understanding, because I think that it is extremely important for all of us to know that even saints got disappointed in those around them. In fact, I'm sure that St. Francis, who was always obedient to the Church and to the Word of God, was extremely disappointed and upset at a Church that seemed to be destroying what he himself had worked so hard to build, to model, and to draw others in this special way of answering God's call. This is so important for all of us as believers today to know, because the Church is such a powerful influence in our lives. It is also such a sensitive and emotional part of our lives. You want to really upset a believer, start messing with their Church, their beliefs, their moral code, and their organization, and you will see a completely different side of even the most passive of people. This all means so much to all of us. If it didn't, you certainly wouldn't be reading these words right now. Men and women have died for this faith. People have been tortured, imprisoned, and made great sacrifices for the Church. You start messing with something as sacred and holy as faith and Church, and it is very easy to get hurt very fast. And yes, I can say that from my own experience, many times over. Sometimes the hardest people for us as believers to deal with, aren't the people outside of the Church, but the very people inside the Church who we are supposed to be in union with and love as brothers and sisters. As St. Francis shows us with his own painful experience of the new Rule, you still don't walk away. You don't give up or quit. You persevere in faith, you keep believing and doing the right thing, and you know and trust that in the end the Truth always comes out. The Holy Spirit is STILL guiding and directing the Church, even when we make mistakes. And we have made some big mistakes over two-thousand years. But you don't give up. You don't quit. St. Francis's perseverance is perhaps his most noble witness to all of us, that he was in this for Jesus. It wasn't about him. He didn't have to have his own way.

And that my brothers and sisters, is a lesson that we all so need today in the Church, and outside of it. So many times all of us can be just like spoiled children. We want our own way, and we don't get it, we are going to pick-up our ball and go home. This is very nature of Protestantism. Martin Luther, Calvin, King Henry VIII, and all of the "reformers" who left, did so because they gave up. It is always easier to walk out the door than to stay and make things better. And the Catholic Church in the United States is steeped also with same attitude. At what point do we acknowledge God's will and God's way as much bigger and more important than our own? So many times, we don't. St. Francis was devastated by what transpired in his own order during these tough days. And this was while he was still alive and still in their midst. He must have wondered what would happen to the brothers when he was gone. But he didn't quit. He didn't give up. And he didn't walk away.

May each one of us remember his example the next time we get upset at the Church or one or some of its members. We're all just working for God. He is really in charge, no matter what we like to tell ourselves. And His Holy Will is being accomplished in our midst, with us or without us. We're not what is most important. He is.

"But seek first the Kingdom of God and His righteousness, and all these things will be given you besides. Do not worry about tomorrow; tomorrow will take care of itself. Sufficient for a day is its own evil."

Matthew 6:33-34

"MESSAGES FROM ASSISI" - DISCUSSION GUIDELINE QUESTIONS

Chapter #16 – Discovering a New Side of Christ / Greccio and the crib

A. Have you ever had to rediscover joy in your faith? What did you do? What was helpful for you in healing the past?

B. St. Francis discovered a new side of Christ. How do we keep discovering more and more about Jesus? What are the things you have done in your life, to open up new roads to faith?

C. Why is evangelization absolutely essential to everything that we are doing as Christians? How does giving the faith to others, increase our own faith?

D. Can you think of other saints, who, like St. Francis of Assisi, went through difficult times caused by the Church itself? What else do these saints have to teach us about faith, about perseverance, and about love?

CHAPTER SEVENTEEN

The Stigmata And
The Beginning Of The End

"All praise be yours, my Lord, through those who grant pardon for love of you; through those who endure sickness and trial. Happy those who endure in peace; by you, Most High, they will be crowned."

St. Francis of Assisi from Canticle of Brother Sun

In the spring of 1224, St. Francis left Greccio, where he had made an impact that would last forever on our celebration of Christmas. He set out for the Portiuncula and a General Chapter meeting of the order. It would be the last time the saint would attend a General Chapter meeting. A few weeks later, perhaps still not finding his place in the order, St. Francis left St. Mary of the Angels for La Verna, a mountaintop hermitage just over a hundred kilometers north of Assisi. La Verna had been given to St. Francis and the Franciscan Order by Count Orlando of Chiusi. St. Francis took with him five of his closest followers: Leo, Angelo, Illuminato, Rufino, and Masseo. Brother Masseo was put in charge of the expedition. St. Francis was very weak, and eventually a donkey was procured for the saint to ride on. This in itself gives us an interesting story, as the farmer who lent his donkey for the saint's use confronted St. Francis, wanting to know if he, indeed, was the great saint that everyone was talking about. St. Francis assured the man that he was Francis of Assisi. The farmer gave the saint a stern warning "to be as good as people say you are" because of his reputation among the people for holiness. *Il Poverino*, in pain and not feeling well, got off the donkey, knelt down on the ground, and kissed the feet of the farmer, thanking him for his honest words.

The trip to La Verna is not easy. Even today with a car, you wind up the mountain for a long while before you finally reach your destination. Walking this, or even riding a donkey, in the late summer heat, would have been a very difficult challenge and would have taken several days. Arriving at the hermitage, Francis and his friends were soon greeted by the Count himself, who brought provisions for the friars and promised them anything that they needed. Here at La Verna, at this time in his life, St. Francis entered even more deeply into prayer, fasting, penance, and spiritual abandonment to God. The saint lived in a small hut under a large tree, separate, but not far from the hermitage where his brothers stayed. Before taking his leave, St. Francis told the five brothers that he knew that his end was near and that they were to stay true to their vows of poverty. They were not to disturb him, and visitors were not permitted. He was to be visited twice a day by Brother Leo, who would bring him bread and water in the morning, and who would pray with him in the evening.

Life went on like this for months. Sometimes Brother Leo would sneak in to check on the saint. At some point during this time, while he was praying on a rocky ledge, St. Francis was given the gift of the stigmata. The five wounds of the Crucified Christ, for whom he had such love and devotion, appeared on the body of the saint! Many say that the actual date was on September 14th, 1224, the Feast of the Exaltation of the Cross. St. Francis had so united his life with that of Christ's that he was even allowed to share in the wounds of our Crucified Savior. This event is one of the most documented events in the saint's life, and yet still today there are doubters who dispute its authenticity. For St Francis, the Stigmata was a very private gift. He allowed no one to see the wounds, but they would be well-documented after his death. Brother Leo, who gave testimony for the saint's canonization, said he was one of the few people who actually saw the wounds. He helped the saint to keep them clean, changed the bandages, and even would helped the saint change his garments, which on many days would become saturated with blood. Brother Rufino and others also gave sworn testimony about the Stigmata. Pope Alexander IV said that he himself had seen the wounds when St Francis was still alive. Indeed, it was intentionally suggested by Pope Alexander that St. Francis remain in seclusion, so as to not become a show. Pope Alexander further said that no additional proof of the presence of the stigmata would ever be needed.

I'm not sure that the modern mind understands that these were real wounds. They were holes in both of his hands, both of his feet, and in his side. They were extremely painful and made it extremely difficult to walk from this point on in his life. St. Bonaventure writes that he had "round black heads on the palm of his hands and on the top of his feet, and he had bent points extruding from the back of his hands and the soles of his feet." This was not a vision or a mirage or a scab or a cut, these were wounds very similar we believe to the ones that Christ would have borne when He was crucified. They went through his hands and feet. And there was a ripped hole in his right side. All of this was kept concealed by the saint and his closest companions. There were new difficulties in caring for St. Francis, both at La Verna, and also later at the hermitage of Le Celle near Cortona. Both of these hermitages were built in the sides of rough mountains. And in both cases, the saint wasn't living in the actual hermitage, but off by himself in even rougher territory and ground. Lots of extra efforts were made to protect the saint and also to care for him.

The reception of the stigmata was really the beginning of the end for St. Francis. His frail, tired body that had so many times also borne illness, harsh penances, fasting, and hard labor, was weakened even further by the loss of blood of the new wounds. In addition, it was not long after this that the saint lost nearly all of his vision. The tough little man from Assisi had taken all the sufferings of the cross that God would give him, and his body had paid dearly for it.

My brothers and sisters, what would happen if each one of us would so conform our lives to that of Jesus Christ that we shared in every part of His being? Would we also eventually have holes in our hands and feet? The stigmata was the logical progression of a life that was deeply connected to the Crucified Christ. St. Francis did what St. John the Baptist also sought to do. He became less and less so that Christ could become more and more of him. The stigmata shouldn't be a shock or surprise to anybody. Nobody had ever gotten that close to the Jesus before. I believe that. And we have some pretty amazing saints in the first twelve-hundred years of Christianity. And yet no saint in the Catholic church accomplished more than what the little poor man from Assisi did in his life. This is why St. Francis is such a great example for all of us. Where he has gone, we too CAN go. But we're not going to do it by just doing the status quo.

St. Francis loved Jesus more and more every single day. He became a mirror of Christ! Why can't we do that? Why are we so happy and content to sit on the sidelines of our faith and our Church, while the game of all eternity is being played right in front of us? It's time for all of us to get in there and get our hands dirty. It's time to go to work. It's time to make a difference and make our Church better. But our faith has got to be a lot more real and a lot more important in our lives for that to happen.

When I was a young boy, my Protestant grandmother gave me a picture-book of the saints. My favorite picture and story in that book was the story of St. Francis of Assisi. There was this beautiful picture on the page with the story of the saint from Assisi, St. Francis, with his arms raised towards a crucifix, receiving the stigmata. The picture had a brilliant blue background with stars, and you could just tell by the expression on the saint's face, who I knew little or nothing about at that time, that he loved Jesus. The story said that St. Francis had received the stigmata while he was praying. I can remember for months after receiving that book, getting on my knees at night beside my bed, and praying as hard as I could, even grunting sometimes, that I could pray like St. Francis. I'd pray and grunt and tense my whole body trying to pray like him. And then I'd look at my hands and feet to see if holes had developed yet. Yeah, it was a silly childish thing. But wanting to be like a man who became so much like Jesus Christ just may be the most mature, more intelligent thing we ever do.

We don't all need to have holes in our hands, our feet, and our sides.

We DO all need to be more like Jesus. May St. Francis's example help all of us to be better!

"Christ Jesus, though He was in the form of God, did not regard equality with God something to be grasped. Rather, He emptied Himself, taking the form of a slave, coming in human likeness; and found human in appearance, He humbled Himself, becoming obedient to death, even death on a cross."

(St. Paul - Letter to the Philippians 2:6-11

"MESSAGES FROM ASSISI" – DISCUSSION GUIDELINE QUESTIONS

Chapter #17 – The Stigmata and the Beginning of the End

A. Why, if Jesus paid the price for our sins, does St. Francis receive the stigmata? Why would God do this to one of his favorite sons? And what does this teach all of us about the importance of our crosses?

B. Why was it so important to St. Francis, his brothers, and even the pope, to conceal St. Francis's stigmata? Why not declare the miracle to the world?

C. How can we unite our sufferings to Christ? Why is it so important to do so? Why is it hard for us to let Christ help us in our times of need?

D. What would we have to do in our lives for the crucified Christ to become as real to us, as he was to St. Francis of Assisi? What's stopping us or getting in the way?

CHAPTER EIGHTEEN

Sister Death And The Transitus

"Be praised, my Lord, for our Sister Bodily Death,
from whom no living man can escape! Woe to those
who shall die in mortal sin! Blessed are those whom
she will find in Your most holy will, for the Second
Death will not harm them. Praise and bless my Lord
and thank Him and serve Him with great humility!

*(St. Francis of Assisi from additional verse added on to the
Canticle of Brother Sun*

St. Francis was back at San Damiano in the spring of 1225 where St. Clare and her sisters were taking care of him. His health had been deteriorating for months following the reception of the stigmata. Also of particular concern was his sight, which seemed to be failing more by the day. That summer, the Pope was living in Rieti, Italy, quite a distance south of Assisi. St. Francis's friend, Cardinal Ugolino and Brother Elias, who was the head of the order at that time, along with several others convinced St. Francis to go Rieti and receive medical treatment for his eyes at the hands of the papal doctors.

The trip itself was difficult. St. Francis made the trip on foot. He wore special shoes that had been made for him by the sisters at San Damiano which compensated for the wounds in his feet from the stigmata. *Il Fioretti* tells a story of the great crowds that came out to greet the saint along the way. Back in Chapter 12, I told the story of

St. Francis's experience at Poggio Bustone when he stopped at the home of a poor priest, where such a great crowd gathered that they trampled the priest's vineyard whose trust in St. Francis's prayer yielded an ample harvest.

The treatment at the hands of the papal doctors was more like torture. And remember, these were the best methods they had in those days. Red hot irons were used to cauterize the muscles around the eyeballs. Done without any anesthetic, the friars accompanying St. Francis had to leave the room when the actual moment came. The treatment had little to no effect. In the winter of 1225 and 1226 St. Francis stayed at a hermitage just north of Siena, because the winter temperatures were more moderate there. In the spring of 1226, as his condition worsened, he was taken to Le Celle—the hermitage just outside of Cortona, about 70 kilometers north of Assisi. The brothers taking care of him brought along two habits for the saint, which they changed and washed constantly to conceal the blood from the stigmata. St. Francis was suffering from the effects of what we today believe was tuberculosis. He was unable to eat any food. His stomach was swollen. And he was spitting up blood. As the end neared, St. Francis asked to be taken back to Assisi and to his beloved Portiuncula to die.

After his conversion, St. Francis became a man without a home, just like the Son of Man in the Gospel Who had no place to lay his head. St. Francis was always moving from town to town, hermitage to hermitage. And so it is somewhat surprising that at the end of his life, that the saint became somewhat nostalgic for his "spiritual home" at St. Mary of the Angels. And yet in another way it made perfect sense to complete the story, the cycle of his life, at the one place that played such a prominent a role in his life. For a brief while after his return, he actually stayed inside the walls of Assisi at the Bishop's residence for protection. An alleged plot by the people of Perugia to come and attack Assisi and steal either the dying saint or his body after death was fully believed by many. It was St. Francis himself who finally demanded to be taken down the hill to the Portiuncula to go home to God.

Leaving the city of Assisi for the last time, the little poor man from Assisi blessed it, saying, "Blessed be you, holy city, for the Lord has chosen you to be a home and abode for all those who in truth will give glory to Him and give honor to His name. And through you, holy city, many souls will be saved, and in you many servants of God will dwell." He couldn't see the white stone and marble buildings cut into the side of the mountain of his hometown and the village where he grew up, but he knew they were there.

It was after several weeks at the Portiuncula, with his brothers around him, in a hut just next to the little church that he had repaired with his own hands, that the servant of God, Francis of Assisi, made the transition from this life to the next. On the evening of October 3rd, 1226, not long after the sun had set, and with his bare body lying directly on the ground, St. Francis died. We can barely imagine the sense of loss for those first Franciscans, for it must have seemed like a light went out of this world. There was great sorrow and mourning. As word spread, all of north central Italy mourned the loss of one of the Church's very best.

St. Francis himself had made peace with death. He knew where he was going. He had worked his whole life to be one with God, and he was looking forward to finally being able to enjoy eternity with Christ whom He loved above all else. He even added a verse to *The Canticle of Creation* or, as it is sometimes called, *The Canticle of Brother Sun*, which is quoted at the beginning of this chapter. He had said all that he wanted to say. He had done all that he could do. His spirit may have still been willing at the age of 44, but the body was definitely done.

I really like the idea of Transitus, or *transition* when it comes to death. The vast majority of our culture sees death as the end. And even if we as believers see and know that there is more coming after death, we still see death as dramatic change. St. Francis saw it as simply a transition to the good that God had promised His faithful people. The Franciscans and many others continue to celebrate the Transitus of St. Francis every October 3rd at sunset. It is a beautiful tradition and makes a nice reminder about "sister" death just about a month before we celebrate All Soul's Day.

We could learn a lot about death also from St. Francis. Death is coming for all of us one day. Before we face that day, even harder than our own dying is facing the death of loved ones around us. We would do well also to make a certain peace with death. Modern culture, most especially in the United States, does all that we can to deny death. We don't even want our dead to look dead, so we paint them up, and cover them up with enough make-up to make us pretend that they are "at rest". We can jog every morning; we can take all the vitamins in the world; we can eat right; we can get eight hours sleep a night. We can even avoid the dangerous areas of our cities and our highways and our world. But one day, ALL OF US are going home to God. It may be in ten minutes. It may be in ten years. It may be in fifty, sixty, or more years (I guess I'm being very hopeful here that at least a few young people will one day read these words). But we are all going to die; it is a good thing to remember that. It's not the end. God's got us covered. But we do have to be prepared for that day, or else it will come like a "thief in the night", as the Bible says. As a Catholic priest, the one most common thing that I have people tell me when they are dying is 'I sure never thought that this would happen to me.' I've had ninety-five year-olds tell me those words! What did they think? Did they really think that they'd live forever? We need to be prepared. St. Francis prepared for most of his life for that trip home to God. It was as easy as going from one room to the next for him.

It can be that easy for us also, IF we know Christ and live intimately with him. Death should never scare a Christian, not even when we lose loved ones. Oh sure, we are going to miss them. Life is different after the loss of those special people in all of our lives. But they don't just disappear. And we won't either.

St. Francis didn't disappear on October 3rd, 1226. We know where he went. The Church, in the canonization process, states clearly "where" he went. We just want to follow "where" he went. And the only way to really do that is to follow Jesus Christ.

"The hour has come for the Son of Man to be glorified. Amen, amen I say to you, unless a grain of wheat falls to the ground and dies, it remains just a grain of wheat; but if it dies, it produces much fruit. Whoever loves his life loses it, and whoever hates his life in this world will preserve it for eternal life. Whoever serves me must follow me, and where I am, there also will my servant be. The Father will honor whoever serves me."

The Gospel of St. John - 12:23-26

"MESSAGES FROM ASSISI" - DISCUSSION GUIDELINE QUESTIONS

Chapter #18 - Sister Death and the Transitus

A. What gave St. Francis of Assisi such a different view of death? How does St. Francis' understanding of death differ from ours today as 21st century Christians?

B. The most important thing that I need to do now, to prepare for my own death, is... what? Why do you say that that's the thing that is most important?

C. What can we do to strengthen the faith of loved ones who are facing death? How can we help them to have a view of death more similar to that of St. Francis?

D. The Franciscans today make it a priority to celebrate the Transitus of St. Francis every year on Oct. 3rd, as a way of remembering St. Francis and his going home to God. How do we remember our loved ones passing from this life? Why is it important to remember? What more could we do to commemorate our loved ones who have gone home before us?

CHAPTER NINETEEN

Preaching, Evangelization, And The Sultan Of Egypt

> "While you are proclaiming peace with your lips,
> be careful to have it even more fully in your Heart.
> Nobody should be aroused to wrath or insult on your
> account. Everyone should rather be moved to peace,
> goodwill, and mercy as a result of your self-restraint."
>
> *(St. Francis of Assisi*

*N*early as soon as St. Francis of Assisi received the call to preach the Gospel to the people of north central Italy, he realized that his call was actually much bigger. And St. Francis greatly desired to take the faith out to the world, as a missionary, and possibly even give his life in the service of the Gospel as a martyr for the faith. By the summer of 1212 this became a major objective of the saint's life. *Il Poverino* had a particular desire to preach the Gospel to the Muslims. To understand this, we have to understand the tensions going on in the world during St. Francis's lifetime. Islamic aggression was threatening many parts of Europe, and the Christian counter-attacks of the Crusades in the Middle East had cost dearly, in terms of life, property, and relations between the two faiths. The hatred that ensued on both sides was the biggest obstacle to peace in the world at that time. St. Francis certainly was also influenced by the particular violence of the most recent crusade, remembered as the "Children's Crusade", where thousands of Europe's youth, encouraged by their parents and their Church, died fighting for their faith. Clearly, St. Francis, the ex-soldier, wanted to bring some kind of peace to the situation.

St. Francis first went to Rome to get Pope Innocent III's permission to enter into the missionary field. It was while he was in Rome for this visit, that he met Lady Jacoba de Settisoli, "Brother Jacoba" as St. Francis called her. Their friendship would last until the saint left this world. He returned to Assisi, and turned the leadership of the order over to Peter Catanii, a member of the order who became the new General Superior of the order, not expecting to ever return. He headed off to the Adriatic and gained passage on ship, which encountered terrible weather and was forced to land in Slavonia. From there, the saint was forced to find a way back to Italy. One story says that he and his companion were stowaways on another ship that also ran into trouble and was delayed at sea. Because of the delay, the food ran out, and St. Francis was forced to come out of hiding and miraculously multiplied the little remaining food that they had, allowing the ship to make it back to Italy. His first effort obviously did not go the way that the saint had planned.

Less than a year later in 1213, St. Francis tried to go over land through France and Spain, to eventually get to Morocco, to preach there. This effort also failed when, according to Thomas of Celano, the saint became seriously ill and was forced to return home. Maybe this wasn't God's plan for St. Francis after all.

Despite his own difficulties in becoming a missionary, in 1217 St. Francis began to send the friars out of Italy to many other parts of the then-known world. Not wanting to ask any of his brothers to do anything that he himself would not do, St. Francis was going to go with a companion to France to preach the Gospel.

This time it was his close friend and advisor, Cardinal Ugolino, who talked him out of it, asking him to stay in Italy and continue his preaching there.

Finally, in 1219, St. Francis resolved once again to take the Gospel to the Muslims, and he left for Egypt with eleven of his brothers. They arrived at Damietta in northern Egypt, right smack in the middle of intense fighting between the crusaders and the Muslims. St. Francis was appalled at the behavior of the crusaders and the Christian armies. It is said that he pleaded with the leaders for them to reconsider their aggression. On August 29th they mounted another attack on Damietta and were soundly defeated, losing thousands of men.

It is at this point that we are not really sure what happened or how it happened. We know that St. Francis sought an audience with the Sultan Malek el Kamil, despite the fact that the Sultan hated Christians. The Sultan, in fact, had offered gold for every Christian head that was brought to him, some sort of meeting did take place. Quite possibly, following the battle at Damietta and the Christian losses, the Sultan might very well have presumed St. Francis to be a negotiator for surrender. *Il Fioretti* tells the account of St. Francis being willing to lay down in a fire that he had built, to show the strength of his faith and his God and challenging one of the Muhammadan priests to do the same. The Sultan, it is claimed, was very impressed by St. Francis's willingness to suffer for another soul and rather disappointed in his own priests for not being willing to do the same thing. This story has gained even more popular support from an unlikely source: Giotto. The Italian artist who did the main frescos in the Upper Basilica of St. Francis in Assisi records the visit with the Sultan as one of his twenty-eight panels. Giotto's painting of this particular scene is unforgettable, although there are many questions about what actually happened. The *Actus* and *Il Fioretti* claim that the Sultan secretly converted to Christianity. There is little evidence for this. What certainly is true is that the Sultan was very taken by St. Francis and by his preaching and commitment to his faith. The sheer fact that St. Francis left the palace with his head that day shows that some change transpired. Today, in the collection of relics at the Sacro Convento in Assisi, you can even view a horn given to St. Francis by the Sultan Malek el Kamil. That's some pretty fancy preaching when you impress your audience enough to let you live when they started out wanting to kill you, AND to give you a gift to show their affection and admiration when all is said and done. Something really special transpired in that meeting. It didn't solve the world's problems, but it did let both sides see with a new understanding.

And maybe that's the legacy that we're supposed to take from this story and from St. Francis's great desire to evangelize. Long before we attempt to "convert" others, how about we respect and try to understand them first? This is not just true with Muslims, but should really be true with everybody. We are so quick to judge. We think we know all about some people all because of the color of their skin, or where they live, or how much money they have OR they don't have. St. Francis risked his life to get into that palace and to tell the Gospel story with fervor, with love, and with understanding. He wasn't trying to beat anybody over the head with his religion. And he wasn't going to water it down, either. But the only Christians that that Sultan knew before St. Francis were the ones coming from foreign land to his country to try and kill him and his people. At least after St. Francis, he had a new idea of Christianity.

How many people today also need a new idea, a new vision, of Christianity, most especially Catholic Christianity? Today we are sent. We all have a Gospel imperative to preach the Gospel - not just missionaries, not just priests, and not just "holy rollers". ALL OF US! What kind of homilies are you giving these days? We can all be better preachers. But what I've found with my preaching? The more we practice it, the better we get.

"The harvest of justice is sown in peace for those who cultivate peace."

James 3: 18

"MESSAGES FROM ASSISI" – DISCUSSION GUIDELINE QUESTIONS

Chapter #19 – Preaching, Evangelization, and the Sultan of Egypt

A. Why was it so important to St. Francis to take the gospel to Egypt and to the Muslims? What must he have had to do in his head and in his heart, to get ready for such an undertaking? How can St. Francis' resolve help and inspire us?

B. Have you ever dealt with someone, like the sultan, who was so terribly angry at the Church? What did you do? How did you respond? How can we better respond to our brothers and sisters who have been hurt by the Church? Do we have a responsibility to do so?

C. While St. Francis' offer to throw himself on the fire as a witness to the faith was just what the sultan needed to know how serious St. Francis was, what does it tell us about the need for courage in witnessing to Christ? In your life, how have you seen Catholic Christians courageously witness to their faith? How can we be more courageous?

D. Who do we know today who might need a "new vision" of the Catholic Church?

CHAPTER TWENTY

The Joy Of St. Francis Of Assisi - Part II

"The joy of St. Francis was not in having nothing. It was in having nothing but God."

St. Bonaventure

---

hree and a-half months ago I began putting down on paper what I was learning from St. Francis of Assisi. The "messages" were profound, comforting, challenging, radical, confirming, peaceful, and life-changing all at the same time. I don't think that I can ever be the same again after this study and reflection. Back in chapter one, we talked about joy being the definitive mark of the life of St. Francis. His joy was infectious. It was what people first and foremost noticed about the saint. And now as we come to conclusion of our time together in these pages, I want to come back to joy. I think we have to at this point. Hopefully, we have come to know at least a little more about the life and the experiences of *Il Poverino* than we did before. That knowledge and experience changes us.

Perhaps it was easier to understand and relate to the joy of a young, enthusiastic spirit on a mission from God. And yet in the story of St. Francis, joy continues to be an extraordinary result of a life lived in communion with God. After years of service, and penance, and many miles, and many varied experiences, that same soul, alas a soul trapped in a rapidly deteriorating body, was still joy-filled.

"The Canticle of Creation" is the best evidence that we have that the joy never left the saint. Devastated by the divisions within his own religious family, weary from a life of hard labor, illness, and sacrifice, and exhausted by the demands that the spread of his reputation and fame had put on his shoulders, it would be easy to understand a great change in the joy of St. Francis. And yet, for St. Francis, the joy and gratitude only seem to increase as his life wound down. He is more grateful to God than ever.

And remember, St. Francis by this time not only had a great devotion to the Cross of Jesus, but after receiving the stigmata, St. Francis knew the experience of the Cross. He had bleeding hands and feet to prove it! The joy never dissipated; it multiplied! He is more in love with Jesus Christ at the end of his life than ever before. And it was Jesus Who is the source and summit of St. Francis's joy.

It is so easy for all of us today to lose our joy. We have so many things weighing on us every day that it is difficult for us to remain joyful or joy-filled. Certainly this is impossible if we are looking to find our joy in the passing "joys" of our world, or if that is our only experience of joy. We have many people today in our world who have no idea what true joy really is. I suppose that to most of them, St. Francis makes little sense. And yet, I can't help but believe that if they could just get a glimpse of the kind of joy that St. Francis had and lived out in his life, that even they would be attracted to what this particular saint had in his life. We are invited to a deeper peace and joy than we can ever begin to imagine. St. Francis found that joy in Jesus in the Sacraments, most especially in the Holy Eucharist, in prayer, in service to the poor, and in living and building up the community of believers.

Where we are finding our peace and joy has EVERYTHING to do with how we are doing. And maybe it truly starts with each of us defining what peace and joy are to us. If you are looking in all the wrong places, you may never find real peace or real joy. Sometimes today, we say we want one thing with our words, but our actions and the desires of our hearts reveal a very different story and give us away. That's never going to work. We've got to be honest about the real desires of our hearts, and we need to be purifying our hearts all the time. Our hearts, just like St. Francis's, hunger for God's love. It is how all of us were "designed and built". St. Francis realized that at the time of his conversion, but it was something that he came to understand more deeply throughout his life.

My concern is that for so many of us as believers today, we may believe that at some points in our lives, if we're lucky, but that it far too often fades in the face of the lure of this world. St. Francis never forgot what his heart was set on. Nor can we! When we fall for the cheap imitation false gods that our world offers, we lose sight of the real prize that God is offering us. It must just leave God completely perplexed at how easily and cheaply we sell out our relationship with Him for so many passing, worthless false gods. Is it any wonder that joy seems to be so missing in our world and in our experience today? Sometimes we just need to remember what's real, what lasts, and what will get us home to Heaven and what will not. And we need to set our hearts on that.

I realize that we have already devoted some time and space to prayer, and yet the single, absolute most essential thing to discovering the joy of St. Francis is prayer. If we're not praying, we aren't going to begin to understand any of this. It is interesting that in the last several years of his life, at La Verna, Cortona, Greccio, and really everywhere he traveled and spent time, St Francis spent more time in prayer than in any other activity. Our problem is that we say that we want to be holy, we claim to want to be a saint like St. Francis, and we certainly would love to experience the miracles in our lives that he did in his, but so few of us are willing to invest the time and effort in becoming real pray-ers. Certainly, the primary source of St. Francis's joy was his prayer life and the sacraments. How unfathomable it would be to the saint that all of us today don't take more advantage of these opportunities for holiness, especially the Mass, the Eucharist! For St. Francis the Eucharist continued the Incarnation of Jesus Christ. It was truly bread turned into the Body of Christ, Who was in fact, God-made-man. For St. Francis, the Eucharist was Jesus showing Himself to modern man every bit as much as He had showed Himself to the Apostles in His real flesh, twelve hundred years earlier in Palestine. Receiving Christ in the Eucharist filled him with joy and allowed him to get closer than any other way to Jesus Christ, Who consumed his soul! Wouldn't it be great if we all walked out of Mass every time feeling that same way?

St. Francis took the time for solitude and reflection. This was a saint who was an inspiration to the entire world, even while he was living. Everybody wanted his time, his presence, and his attention. And yet St. Francis was keenly aware of just how much he needed to get away by himself, not just for prayer, but also for reflection and solitude. Sometimes, to stay focused, to stay on track, and to keep your joy, you have to have some time and space to remember what you're doing and why you're doing it. St. Francis wasn't afraid to take that time or make that time for himself or for his brothers. Perhaps our difficulty in finding and keeping joy in our lives is very much linked to the fact that we don't take time for quiet, for reflection, and for solitude. We always have to have noise and busyness going on around us at all times. We don't like to be alone. We don't take the time to think about what we're doing, when we pile up so much to do! All of this makes joy more and more difficult to find in our lives today. St. Francis points a way for us. We would do well to pay attention to the message he is trying to teach us.

Today, to many believers and non-believers, St. Francis was just a nice, gentle guy who we like to have standing in our backyards in the middle of our gardens. The little man from Assisi was a peaceful man, and he was a man of great compassion and concern for others. And yet "gentle" is a very difficult word to apply to a saint who lived so many aspects of his life in an "all-or-nothing" fashion. St. Francis in many ways was an extremist. He didn't do things part-way. He certainly could be very hard on himself, but also on others in calling them to Christ. Undoubtedly there were those in the thirteenth century who ran into the forcefulness of our saint and who would have never referred to him as "gentle", including a few bishops and at least one Pope. St. Francis may have been gentle, but he was not a push-over. You can be joy-filled AND still stand up for what you believe in. You can be in conflict with someone else and still keep your joy, if you have peace about where you are at in the conflict. St. Francis is an immensely complex person. He was passionate. He loved life. He deeply loved and cared for those around him. And he could also be very demanding and very uncompromising, and he would not back down just to make someone feel better. Sometimes, to have real joy, you have to "stick to your guns". Was he gentle? In his joy and peace and kindness to others, he perhaps appeared gentler than he actually was. Certainly in art and paintings, one calls to mind Giotto's *St. Francis Preaching to the Birds*, St. Francis certainly appears very meek and gentle. St. Francis's gentleness was built on a foundation of strength that allowed him to accomplish amazing things during his lifetime.

Joyful praise and service of God is at the very heart of Franciscan spirituality. We respond to God's love revealed to us when God was born of the Virgin Mary and took on and shared our human experience in poverty and humility. God's actions give us joy and gratitude to live the same kind of love for Him and for others, especially the poor. The "joy" of St. Francis influenced everything in his life, his order, and his world. What kind of joy do you have in your life? And how is your joy being played out in the way that you live? It is amazing the difference that joy can make. Watch how contagious it can be in your own life.

"I have told you this so that my joy might be in you and your joy might be complete. This is my commandment: love one another as I have loved you."

The Gospel of St. John 15: 11-12

"MESSAGES FROM ASSISI" - DISCUSSION
GUIDELINE QUESTIONS

Chapter #20 - On St. Francis' Love of Lady Poverty

A. If we don't already have it, how can we develop a sensitivity, or preference, for the poor? How does a preference for the poor get lived out every day in the Church?

B. St. Francis of Assisi was so concerned about money, property, and possessions getting in the way of his relationship with God. Aren't there also a lot of other things too, that keep us from God? How do we know them? What do we do about them?

C. What does being "poor in spirit" mean to you? How is being "poor in spirit" different from the world's version of poverty? Was St. Francis' version of poverty too strict for others?

D. Why is materialism now considered one of the most accepted heresies in the world today? Why is it still not o.k. for Christians to just keep acquiring more things?

E. Are we afraid to live without our wealth? If we did have to choose, what would it be? God or our things?

CHAPTER TWENTY-ONE
On St. Francis's Love Of Lady Poverty

"When you see a poor person, you are looking at a mirror of the Lord And his poor mother."

St. Francis of Assisi

ven before his conversion, St. Francis of Assisi had a special affection and sensitivity to the poor. He was always very generous and giving towards all that he encountered. Throughout his teen years and young adulthood prior to conversion, it was usually Francis who picked up the bill for food and wine and whatever was needed to have a good time with his companions. Pietro Bernardone's thriving cloth business enabled this luxury and generosity. Certainly on more than one occasion, young Francis was reprimanded by both of his parents for his extravagant spending habits. And yet, Francis was a hard worker. He knew the value of money. He spent many hours working in his father's store and was popular with the customers. He and his friends were good for business. Quite possibly, Pietro didn't mind his son's lavish spending and generosity. But the truth is, he and his wife, Pica, never really demanded that Francis stop his spending and giving habits. Francis, from very early on, enjoyed giving to the poor and those in need. It seemed to give him great pleasure even when he was very young.

St. Bonaventure, an early Franciscan and source of information on St. Francis's life who became the third Superior General of the order, tells us that a love of the poor was born in St. Francis. He promised himself that he would never refuse anyone who asked from him in the name of God. Again it is Bonaventure who recounts the story of how only once did young Francis refuse to come to the aid of someone begging for help. Young Francis was assisting a customer in his father's store when a beggar entered, asking for help in the name of God. Francis angrily dismissed the beggar and demanded that he leave. Embarrassed by his behavior and regretting his words and actions at once, St. Francis ran through the streets of Assisi until he found the beggar and gave him assistance. Francis reasoned that if the poor man had come asking for help in the name of one of his friends, he would not have hesitated to help him. Instead, the beggar came in the name of his Lord Jesus Christ, and Francis had refused him. The young Saint vowed that it would never happen again.

When Francis got a little older, and most especially when his father was away on business, young Francis would ask those preparing their meals to make more than what was really needed, so as to ensure that there would be plenty for the poor who would come begging later in the evening. It is recorded that while his father never seemed to notice the requests or the extra portions, St. Francis's mother was very aware of her son's penchant for giving away their food, and she greatly admired his compassion.

It is no coincidence then that Francis's encounter with a poor knight near Spoleto is the spark that ignites his conversion. The knight, who is near naked in appearance and has nothing, elicits a great respect and admiration from Francis. And he either asks him for some assistance or the Saint simply takes off his shiny new armor and gives it to him, along with his mighty new horse. But this singular act of generosity sets into motion the total conversion of our Saint, from the dreams of knighthood on the battlefield to seeking the glory of God in complete and total poverty.

One of the clearest aspects of St. Francis's life during and after his conversion was that all the extravagant things, and most especially the money, that he had so taken advantage of and enjoyed throughout his younger years, all had to go. They were distractions keeping him from God. Jesus's instructions to the rich young man in the Gospel (see Mt. 19: 16 -24 "If you wish to be perfect, go and sell what you have, give the money to the poor, and come and follow me") were taken quite literally by St. Francis. The words went right along with what he himself had experienced in life. Long before Francis took of his clothes at the piazza of the bishop's residence and returned them to his father, he was already stripping himself of his possessions and his money. The famous showdown with his father, which is another of the scenes of his life recounted in Giotto's frescos in the Upper Basilica in Assisi, was just the logical next step in St. Francis being led, concerning the value of material goods. Francis renounces his earthly father and all of his earthly things, in exchange for the things of Heaven. For St. Francis, it is what he must do to live only for Christ. It was as clear as a full moon-lit Assisi night.

It is also worth noting here that it was not enough for St. Francis to serve the poor and those in need. He was called to become poor and needy. St. Francis became more and more aware of the fact that Jesus in the Incarnation had so humbled Himself, had given up so much to become one of us, that the only way to truly understand what Christ had done in becoming poor for us, was to become poor himself. Thus our Saint went from giving from his own wealth to the poor, to becoming poor himself and giving absolutely everything to God and to those in need. This created the complete reliance on God that St. Francis so believed that we all need to have. For Francis, the poorest of the poor are the perfect teachers of authentic faith! Thomas of Celano writes that St. Francis became one of them, thinking only of sharing in their life of privations. He loved poverty itself.

St. Francis referred to his new way of life as a marriage to Lady Poverty. And Lady Poverty, contrary to most of our images of poverty today, was a beautiful image that St. Francis had of a complete abandonment of oneself to God. Like the Gospels' complete reversal of values that shows up so often in Sacred Scriptures, St. Francis's notion of poverty was that it provided the only true way to everlasting riches and treasure. St. Francis demonstrated to all of us how this worked by rigidly living this poverty out in his own life. His radical commitment to living under even harsher conditions than the poorest of the poor to make room for Christ, changed his life and brought many others to

Jesus and salvation. It is perhaps the highest value that St. Francis had in his life and one that he clung to vehemently throughout his life and ministry. As the Franciscan Order grew, the commitment to total and complete poverty became a major point of contention within the order, even before St. Francis left this world. And this would eventually lead, a hundred years later, to the Pope's denouncing Franciscan poverty as "too strict" and as an effort to hold Franciscans to a poverty that was "beyond what Christ Himself lived and taught".

Today those in the Franciscan Order continue to struggle with exactly how to live out their vow of poverty in every different branch of the now- fragmented order. St. Francis's life and his teaching on poverty continue to challenge not only the Franciscan Order but all of us who authentically seek to follow Christ and who are inspired by the Little Poor Man of Assisi.

The heart of the matter is how can all of us, like St. Francis, give ourselves completely to Jesus Christ, while we are living in the material world? St. Francis found that nearly all things got in the way. And remember, he would have known a lot about this, having grown up with fairly luxurious lifestyle. St. Francis gets rid of it all. He reduces his life down to its barest essentials, and then takes on the least of the minimum. He exchanges his finest clothes for the lowest rags of the poor. How many times did St. Francis take off his own tattered garments and exchange them for even more deteriorated ones from the poor? He exchanges fine food and excellent wine and the most delicious of treats that he enjoyed in his younger life for the most repulsive scraps of food and garbage that we can't even bear to imagine as we read the words on this page. And again, Francis's preference was always for the very lowest, even in his Order and amongst his brothers. St. Francis would consciously seek out the smallest piece of bread or the one with the most mold on it; the oldest, most spoiled vegetables and fruit; and the most pathetic scraps of meat that were left over. St. Francis exchanges the fine bed and comfortable accommodations of his parents' home for the most uncomfortable accommodations of living on the street or in the fields. To see the rough, uneven, and uncomfortable places hewn out of rock where St. Francis is believed to have slept at the Hermitage above Assisi or at the first home of the Franciscans at Rivotorto, is startling. St. Francis didn't just do poverty; he accepted it. He embraced it. He did poverty to the extreme, to the maximum!

What was he trying to tell us? What was God using this most-prized instrument of all His human sons and daughters to try to get across to us? It is far too easy to say, "Well, that's what God wanted for St. Francis." By dismissing St. Francis's poverty as only for him, or even for the strictest Franciscans, I think we miss the point of the lesson. And there is a message here for all of us: Who or what is "god" in our lives? The first commandment is "I am the Lord your God, you shall not have false gods BEFORE Me." What are the "false" gods we have in our lives today?

Consider for just a moment our "problems" today. Our addictions to both materialism and consumerism and St. Francis's emphasis on poverty and sacrifice is not just good advice, but an absolutely essential message for the salvation of our souls! The power of goods, and things, and wealth in the thirteenth century was one thing; at the beginning of the twenty-first century, boosted by advertising, greed, and an insatiable appetite for the new and the better, it is completely out of control. When our lives, and most especially our souls, are prioritized by our belongings and our wealth, we are completely out of control. Perhaps this is St. Francis's greatest challenge to us today! Most of us will never take a vow of poverty in our lives. Nor are we all called by the Lord to do so. But all of us are called to make the Lord the center of our lives and our being. That becomes a very difficult thing to do when we are so worried about acquiring things, and taking care of our things, and not losing our things, that we scarcely find time for God and the matters of the soul. All of us would do very well indeed to heed the warning that St. Francis's life and poverty gives to us. St. Francis knew what he was talking about. He had wealth, and he freely chose to give it all up to receive the everlasting wealth of the Good News of Jesus Christ! Isn't it interesting that St. Francis never ran back to his old way of life? Certainly he remembered the comforts, the delicious foods, and the worry-free life that money affords. And yet St. Francis found something so much better that he never looked back. I think most of us are afraid that if we really give up our "things", or even give up our love of our things, that somehow we will be lost without them or without that love and attachment. God promises us otherwise. It is not our lack of things that is the real issue. The real issue is our fear and desperate need for acceptance in this world. We are scared to death of exactly what God might actually do with us if He really was the most important thing in our lives.

And so, if we're not all going to become Franciscans (and maybe I'm thinking at this point that all of us as Catholic Christians need to have a little Franciscan in us!), what exactly are we to do? How do we even begin to get ourselves out of our materialistic mindsets? We can start by setting some limits. The line that disappeared from our cognitive abilities is when and what is enough. Our desire for more of the world has made us obsessed, greedy, fat, and addicted to the acquisition of more. We walk into our homes and we don't see the nice furniture, we don't see the latest electronics, we don't see the comforts and amenities that we take for granted, that a century ago, the richest and most powerful men and women in the world did not have or enjoy. Instead we walk in and all we can think about is newer, and bigger, and faster, and better. Let's start out with being grateful and happy for what we do have and acknowledging far more often just how truly blessed we are. That's how we can start.

And then, to truly take on the values of our world, Madison Avenue, and the media, we're going to have fight attachment with detachment. Our things are just things. They break. They get stolen. They wear out and become obsolete. And remember, we are taking not a single thing home with us to God except our souls! Now tell me about how important and necessary it is for you to have that bigger TV, or that newer car, or that latest exercise equipment. We've got to quit filling our heads, our hearts, and unfortunately, yes, even our souls, with the things that we think are going to make us happy, and yet never will. We've got to change our own priorities.

St. Francis did that and when he pulled all of the things, all of the money, and all of the prestige that went along with the things and the money, out of the way, he found a very real God Who wanted to do amazing things with him, but first he had to detach himself from everything that was keeping God hidden. St. Francis divested himself of everything that kept him from Jesus. Isn't that exactly what the rich young man from the parable wasn't able to do? The rich young man from the Gospel certainly never chose to acquire his wealth and possessions over God. He probably didn't think about it at all as he gained his wealth. By his birth, by his family, by his own work and enterprising spirit, he had become a very wealthy individual. But when the time came for him to follow God and become what God wanted him to be, the rich young man wasn't able to give up what he had become quite accustomed to over time. He was afraid; he couldn't imagine life without his wealth. And that's exactly how wealth, and materialism, and even consumerism, wreaks its havoc in our lives. All of us are far wealthier than we'd ever dare to admit. Is our wealth keeping us from God? Yes, it probably is. The only question that is left is: what are we going to do about it?

"DO NOT HAVE JESUS CHRIST ON OUR LIPS AND THE WORLD IN YOUR HEARTS."

St. Ignatius of Antioch

"MESSAGES FROM ASSISI" - DISCUSSION GUIDELINE QUESTIONS

Chapter #21 - The Canticle of Creation

A. Why is gratitude so important? How can we be more grateful people? What does gratitude do for us?

B. How can we, like St. Francis of Assisi, use the promises of God, to stay positive in this life? What does God promise us that should help us to not lose hope?

C. What does the perspective of the unity of all creation offer to us today? How can it help to make our world a better place at this time?

D. If we were to write a poem/song/canticle at the end of our life, what do you want your canticle to say? What would sum up your gratitude to God?

CHAPTER TWENTY-TWO
The Canticle Of Creation

"Most high, all-powerful God, all good Lord! All praise is yours, all glory, all honor, and all blessing."

St. Francis of Assisi

The spring of 1225 was a particularly difficult time for St. Francis. His body was weak and in constant pain. The loss of blood from the stigmata had taken its toll. And the constant pain in his hands and feet was relentless. His eyesight continued to deteriorate and the remedies for his blindness were in almost every case worse than the problems caused by his lack of sight. Later that summer, St. Francis would endure the cauterization of the muscles around his eyes with red-hot irons. The tensions within the Franciscan Order over poverty and specifically the ownership of property, continued to escalate also, bringing the saint more tension, worry, and heartbreak. After returning to Assisi and the Portiuncula, it was clear that St. Francis was going to need near constant care. St. Clare and her sisters took St. Francis in and cared for him at San Damiano. St. Clare made special gloves and socks to protect the wounds of the stigmata. A make-shift hut was constructed on the convent grounds for him to live in. The hut was modeled after the one that the brothers had built for him at St. Mary of the Angels. St. Clare and the sisters thought that it would be a place of great peace and rest for St. Francis. This was not to be, due to an infestation of mice. The sisters and St. Francis himself would try to scatter the mice away, but the more they drove out, the more the little hut was full of them. They were in the walls and all over the floor. They would jump up on the little table with the saint's food on it. Since St. Francis was lying on a mat on the ground, the mice would also scurry over his body and on several occasions over his face! Exhausted, in great pain, blind, and tempted to despair, St. Francis cried out to God for mercy. It was then and there, after receiving a promise from God that his sufferings would be nothing in light of the great joy that awaited him in Heaven, that St. Francis found not only peace, but ecstatic joy! St. Francis was reborn for the final months of his life. His despair was turned to great gratitude and appreciation for all that God had done for him and for all of us. And there was no greater expression of that re-birth, than the *Canticle of Brother Sun* or as we know it more often today, "The Canticle of the Creatures."

St. Francis wrote a most extraordinary song of praise! He thanked God for his existence. He gave thanks for all of nature and life. He expressed his gratitude for God's victory over death and evil. He praised God for the sun, the moon, the earth, the sky, fire, water and the wind. All was seen as gift from God! This was quite a turn-around from the despairing man, racked with pain, lying on the floor of a hut with mice running all over him! And he was praising God for a creation that he could no longer see or experience. Truly, this one of his last works of his incredible life is also one of St. Francis's very best!

With one poem/song St. Francis would revolutionize poetry and literature forever. If our saint had done nothing else in his lifetime, St. Francis could be remembered for this single contribution to the literary world, such is the impact of "The Canticle of the Creatures", not only on Italian literature, but on all literature and poetry. All Italian school children are still required to memorize "The Canticle" when they are young. It brims over with love and gratitude. It is as though St. Francis is taking the entire Gospel message and summing it up in a song of thanksgiving. And make no mistake about it, this poem was meant to be sung. St. Francis always loved to sing, even before his conversion. "The Canticle of the Creatures" becomes his greatest hymn, the song of his life, given freely back to God.

"The Canticle of the Creatures" expresses the unity of all creation. We are all related to one another, and we are all related to everything. Everything has its purpose; everything is to work together for the glorification of the Lord. That unity that St. Francis himself felt so much a part of, was all part of God's plan and His gift to all of us. God was in fact redeeming all of His creation and creatures. All of creation is sacred! All of creation was being used by God to accomplish His goal. The Canticle celebrates this and reminds us that this is what life is all about! Our fraternity as creatures binds us together in the love of God and makes us a part of a bigger whole: God's family! St. Francis knew that love and that sense of being connected well. In "The Canticle of the Creatures" he invites all of us to be part of it.

One glance at "The Canticle of the Creatures," and you don't even have to get to the line "All praise be yours, my Lord, through Sister Earth, our mother" to realize that "The Canticle of the Creatures" was destined to become the favorite prayer of environmentalists and all of our green, tree-hugging brothers and sisters. In fact, it is largely attributed to "The Canticle of the Creatures" that St. Francis has become the Patron saint of the modern environmental movement. St. Francis did love nature and did spend a whole lot of time outside, and he did call all of us to live moderately, even simply, not using any more of the earth's precious resources than we need. And St. Francis did have a love for animals, except apparently mice, which he considered to be a plague from the devil. But to try to turn our saint into some kind of thirteenth century environmentalist and crusader for the protection of the earth would be wrong. St. Francis was head-over-heels in love with Jesus Christ and with sharing the Gospel message. The Gospel itself does demand that we respect creation, that we not be selfish or greedy when it comes to the earth's goods, and that all creation works together for the glory of God. However, it is frustrating to see St. Francis reduced to being a "holy environmentalist". This modern tendency so misses the point of what this holy man is trying to teach us and connects him up with a political cause that the saint himself might not have endorsed. It's too simple to just say that St. Francis loved the earth and loved animals; there's more to his story than that. And "The Canticle of the Creatures" proves it!

Do you think that I am exaggerating this point? Just try to find a statue of St. Francis of Assisi where he is NOT holding a bird or standing next to a wolf! It is very difficult. The truth is that the real St. Francis was much more connected to the crucifix than he was to birds or wolves. Have you seen a statue of St. Francis of Assisi with a crucifix? I have, but they are hard to find. My fear is that some have turned *Il Poverino* into an earlier, Catholic version of Doctor Dolittle. Even our smallest children deserve to know more about this saint than that.

And thus, it was once again at San Damiano that God spoke to and through His servant Francis of Assisi. It was always San Damiano that had such an impact on St. Francis's vocation. It was to the cave at San Damiano that St. Francis had run and hidden following his imprisonment in his father's house. It was here that the crucifix, the Cross of San Damiano, had spoken to him and told him to "rebuild the Church". It was here, down below Assisi, that he and his first followers had rebuilt the little church. And it was here at this time, that his follower, Clare, had built her community that cared for him and witnessed to God's everlasting love for him. San Damiano was the perfect place to write his greatest song of praise of God.

"You are robed in power, You set up the mountains by Your might. You still the roaring of the seas, the roaring of their waves, and the Tumult of the people. Distant people stand in awe of your marvels; east and west You make resound with joy! You visit the earth and water it, make it abundantly fertile. God's stream is filled with water; with it You supply the world with grain. Thus do You prepare the earth!"

Psalm 65:7-10

"MESSAGES FROM ASSISI" - DISCUSSION GUIDELINE QUESTIONS

Chapter #22 - St. Francis of Assisi and the Eucharist

A. What can each of us do to keep Mass from becoming "routine" in our lives?

B. How does the honor and respect that we show as Church and Church leaders, influence and promote devotion to the Holy Eucharist?

C. What can we do as Catholic Christians to get more out of the Mass for ourselves and for our community? What more can we do to build up respect, devotion, and commitment to the Holy Eucharist?

D. How has the Eucharist empowered you to live out your faith? How has your own experience with Mass and the Eucharist helped you to understand the life of the saints and their commitment to the Eucharist?

CHAPTER TWENTY-THREE

St. Francis And The Eucharist

"The heart of (Tertiaries') prayer is the Eucharist, in which they share with other Christians the renewal of their union with Their Lord and Savior in His sacrifice, remember His death and receiving His spiritual food."

The Principles of the Third Order of the Society of St. Francis of Assisi, Day Fifteen

As with most of the Catholic saints, I suppose that it is no surprise that St. Francis of Assisi found great comfort and spiritual sustenance in the Eucharist, and recommended regular Holy Communion to all of his followers. What might surprise us is just how much the Mass meant to St. Francis of Assisi. So many times all of us as modern Catholics take the Mass for granted. Many come and go at Mass as they please because they truly don't understand what they're missing. Our saint didn't just go to Mass to put in his time or to fulfill his obligation. He went to Mass because the Jesus that he received in the Holy Eucharist was the very One who enabled the young man from Assisi to do incredible things in his life and changed him forever. St. Francis of Assisi was in love with Jesus Christ! There was no way for the saint to get closer to Jesus than in receiving Him, Body, Blood, Soul, and Divinity in the Holy Eucharist. St. Francis's active life, his never-ending service to the poor and sick, his continual preaching of the Gospel everywhere he went, and his leadership of an ever-growing new order in the Catholic Church, never were more important in the saint's daily schedule than going to Mass as often as he could. What a challenge to all of us today who sometimes like to pretend that we are too busy to go to Mass. St. Francis—with all that he was doing—was never too busy for Mass. Perhaps he and so many of our greatest saints were great saints because they never missed an opportunity to receive Jesus into their lives.

St. Francis of Assisi, who was an ordained Deacon of the Church but not a priest, had to constantly seek out priests to offer Mass for him and his brothers. From the very beginning of the order, several priests were attracted to the Franciscan life, and St. Francis himself did send worthy brothers to seminary to be trained as priests and come back to serve the order. The Mass and the Eucharist gave life to St. Francis and the Franciscans. As a child, St. Francis attended Sunday Mass with Pica and his father when he was home. As a young man, the words of the Gospel of Matthew proclaimed at Mass and explained by the priest in his homily, were the direct challenges that led to St. Francis's conversion. The early brothers could never be too far removed from the location of a church or chapel that offered regular Mass. Even toward the end of his life, when he was sick and unable to serve in active ministry, the Mass was still the most important part of his day, and he oftentimes had one of the brothers who was a priest pray the Mass at his bedside. This was done for him even on the day that he died.

Why was this such a big deal to St. Francis? Why, too, does the Catholic Church even up unto today make such a huge thing out of Holy Communion? It is because for St. Francis—as it is supposed to be for the entire Catholic Church—Jesus, Who reveals Himself to us in bread, is the exact same Jesus Who two-thousand years ago showed Himself to the Apostles in human flesh. For St. Francis, the Holy Eucharist and the Incarnation of the Christ are the same mystery. If we can't see and experience Jesus in the Eucharist, how are we ever going to experience Him when He comes in any number of other disguises? Does a carpenter from Nazareth really look any more like God than does a morsel of bread? The Eucharist goes way beyond what things look like to what they actually are. Jesus was a whole lot more than just a nice Jewish carpenter. The Apostles believed Him to be the Messiah, God, and our Savior. So too do we as Catholics, in the good company of St. Francis of Assisi and the saints, also believe that morsel of bread becomes so much more than just bread when it is consecrated at Mass. We believe that it becomes the Body of Christ!

That recognition of Jesus in the Breaking of the Bread, as Luke's Gospel (Chapter 24:13-35) would put it, would become absolutely essential to St. Francis' ministry to the poor and preaching of the Good News. To preach Jesus to the poor, the hungry, the sick, and the lost, St. Francis would need to be able to see Jesus in each person that he came in contact with and desired to serve. St. Francis was never just being a nice guy and just trying to help out because he was concerned about this leper, or that homeless person, or that hungry child. St. Francis of Assisi was loving them because for him, they were Jesus! Just as he had learned to see Jesus revealed in the Eucharist, and to love and to serve Him there, so too did he learn to see Jesus in those he ministered to every day.

The Passion of Christ's sacrifice led St. Francis to be more passionate in his love for Jesus and the Eucharistic sacrifice that is offered on altars all over the world at every Mass. For Christ and for St. Francis, all true love involved suffering and sacrifice. Without the willingness to sacrifice, both would say that love wasn't true love. In the Eucharist, St. Francis found true consolation for his deep faith that God so loved him that Christ had died on that Cross for our sins. And it led him to want to give up even more to grow in his own love. How could you hold anything back from a God Who held nothing back for us?

In the Gospel of John (6:56) Jesus tells His followers: "Whoever eats my flesh and drinks my blood remains in me and I in him." St. Francis understood that verse. He realized that in the Holy Eucharist he was given the opportunity to have Jesus with him, inside of him, and empowering him each time he received the Sacrament. It was THAT important! We need to believe more in the power of what we receive at Mass. It was St. Pio of Pietrelcina who wrote that if we really believed that the Eucharist was the Body and Blood of Christ, we shouldn't be genuflecting or bowing at Mass, we should be on our faces before the presence of the Living God! What would it take for us to love Jesus more in the Holy Eucharist? How can we have a better appreciation of the Mass as so many of the saints did?

"Take this all of you and eat it. This is my Body Which will be given up for you."

Jesus at the Last Supper

"MESSAGES FROM ASSISI" - DISCUSSION GUIDELINE QUESTIONS

Chapter #23 - Assisi and the World of St. Francis

A. How was St. Francis of Assisi influenced by his "hometown"? How do our surroundings influence all of us, even when it comes to our faith?

B. What would be the place that you would like to see, or visit, or go back to in Assisi, that you believe would help you to experience the "real" St. Francis? Where in Assisi do you think that St. Francis would feel most at home today?

C. Almost all of the main branches of the Franciscan Order, or family, have some presence in the little town of Assisi. Why is this important do you think, that the followers of St. Francis and St. Clare stay connected to Assisi? What benefits does the order receive from staying in Assisi?

D. How does where we live and are from inspire us and challenge us to be better? And how does where we live and are from pull us down and limit us from becoming what God wants us to be?

CHAPTER TWENTY-FOUR
Assisi And The World Of St. Francis

"In Assisi, I came to know the Creator and truly did feel in solidarity with all of humanity. And that knowledge and feeling stayed with me after I left the holy little city that sits on a hill. It burns within me. But I must keep it burning. Each day, as best I can, I try and stoke the flames within me, the flames of the spirit of the eternal shrine that is Assisi."

Gerald Thomas Straub - from his book "The Sun and Moon Over Assisi"

To say that Assisi and the spirit of St. Francis have affected many lives is an understatement. Millions of lives have been changed by this small town on the western slope of Mount Subasio. Even the briefest of visits to the walled city can have the most profound effect on the visitor. This is one of the reasons why when you ask so many modern travelers to Italy what one place you would most like to go back to, nearly always they will say Assisi.

Beginning in the mid-1990's I have had the opportunity to lead pilgrimages to Italy for our high school students. Every two years in June, 25 to 35 high school students and some of their parents and youth ministers travel with me to Italy. We first go to Assisi, and stay there for six days, seeing Florence, Siena, and Orvieto. And then we travel down to Rome for a week and visit the Holy City and points of interest south of Rome. Every pilgrimage when we get to Rome, the high school folk want to go back to Assisi. I also hear this almost unanimously from the adults, but it is a bigger surprise from the youth. "Don't you want to see the Pope, and the Vatican and the Coliseum?" I ask. And they do, of course, they just miss the peace and the spirit of Assisi.

One visit to Assisi at any time and for any duration and even the most jaded traveler will have to admit that there is something very special about this small medieval city. It seems most natural that this would have been the birthplace of both St. Francis and St. Clare. There is a peace, a calmness, and even a certain joy contained within its walls and throughout its curvy, hilly streets. It takes very little imagination to see a young Francis or Clare walking these streets, praying, singing, and begging for the poor. Their spirit is still so alive even in modern Assisi.

And yet it was here on the side of this mountain, back in the thirteenth century, that God changed the hearts of its young people and began a spiritual revolution that would in fact change and renew the entire Catholic Church. Something had happened to Francis, to Clare, to Francis' friends, and to Clare's sisters, and to so many of their companions and neighbors. Their hearts were converted to Christ! Was it the town or the location or the streets? No, of course it wasn't. And yet it is hard to say that the incredible beauty and raw natural setting of Assisi didn't have anything to do with it. With its flowering hillside meadows, its dark green forest-covered hills, its brilliant blue skies, its pink and white marble streets and buildings, and the most extraordinary sunsets to the west, overlooking the Spoleto valley, you get the impression that God's natural gifts to Assisi quite easily led its young people to consider God in all of His wonder!

Assisi is located in the Umbrian region of Italy. It is in the province of Perugia. A community was first settled in Assisi around the year 1000 BC. Immigrants had come up from the Tiber valley and stopped at this small, fortified settlement on high ground. These immigrants became known as the "Umbrians". By 450 BC their community was taken over by the Etruscans. And by 295 BC, with the Battle of Sentinum, the Romans took control of Assisi. The Romans had major accomplishments while they were in charge. The city wall was built. The Forum, today known as the Piazza Del Commune, was built. A theater, an amphitheater, and the Temple of Minerva, the remains of which today are the church of Santa Maria Minerva, were also built by the Romans. In 283 AD, the city was converted to Christianity by Saint Ruffino, the first bishop of Assisi and the first saint to come from the town. St. Ruffino was martyred for his faith, being drowned at Costano. In 545 AD, Assisi was destroyed by the Ostrogoths under the leadership of King Tolila. Then the Lombards took control of Assisi, under the Frankish Duchy of Spoleto. In the 11th Century, Assisi became an independent Ghibelline community. This made the city vulnerable to Guelph Perugia, which began centuries of wars, battles, feuds, and skirmishes with its neighbors just to the north. It was in one of these battles/ skirmishes at Ponte San Giovanni, that a nineteen-year-old Francesco Bernardone was captured and put into prison in Perugia for ransom. That capture triggered the conversion of St. Francis, which would eventually put Assisi on the world map forever. In 1253, a mere twenty-seven years after the death of St. Francis, the Basilica of St. Francis was dedicated in Assisi.

The thirteenth century found Assisi under Papal rule. In 1187, in an uprising of the new merchant class, the Rocca Maggiore was attacked and severely damaged. A very young Francis and his father may very well have been involved in that uprising. In 1367 the fortress was re-built under papal orders. The fourteenth century sees Assisi fall under the rule of Perugia and several despots. The city declined until the Black Death struck Assisi in 1348. The fifteenth century saw Assisi once again under papal control and protection. In 1569 construction was begun on Santa Maria degli Angeli down below Assisi, to protect the remains of the Portiuncula and the Chapel of the Transitus. Assisi has grown by the year to be one of the world's most popular pilgrimage sites. And today millions of visitors pass through Assisi every year.

Ever since Saint Ruffino converted Assisi to Christianity, faith has been a very important part of the town's life. Even before St. Francis and St. Clare, Assisi with blessed with many beautiful churches and chapels. Saint Mary Majors is the oldest of the big churches still in existence today. The Cathedral of San Ruffino, where the saint's remains are kept in the main altar, remains in existence but in a newer church built over the original one. San Ruffino is where both St. Francis and St. Clare were baptized into the faith.

The newer basilicas of St. Francis and St Clare, both major attractions in modern Assisi, have their own histories. St. Clare's was built over the remains of St. George's church, where young St. Francis went to school, not far from where his family lived. It was at St. George's where the Bishop of Assisi lived that St. Francis took off his clothes and gave them back to his father, Pietro. The Basilica of St. Francis, with the final resting place of our saint in its crypt, was built on the side of the mountain on the northwest corner of Assisi. In St. Francis's time, this was both a dump and a burial place for the poor. Very few people in the thirteenth century would ever have gone out there for any reason. I think that St. Francis would have really liked that this place was where he was going to be buried and his basilica built. Today the Basilica of St. Francis is the most popular visitor's destination in Assisi.

Today about two thousand people have permanent residency and live within the city walls of Assisi. Many of them have lived there for years. Most of them are or have been involved in the tourist/hospitality business. Many of them are also religious priests, brothers, and sisters, who are assigned there for awhile, and then come and go. Today thousands more Assisians live outside the walls of the city in the surrounding area. Assisi is basically a large town. Most of the permanent residents know each other and each others' business. One can imagine the stories going around about the young Bernardone boy's craziness or the scandal of Clare's midnight escape from her father's house. Assisi, like all towns, still has its legends, characters, and stories.

But this little town is different. Assisi is holy ground. For from this small community God brought forth two saints who changed the entire church. The Franciscans and the Poor Clares continue to change lives even today, in the name and spirit of their founders. It is a beautiful legacy. It is an extraordinary place.

I would pray that every Catholic would get the chance to go to

Assisi one day. It is a simple little town. And Assisi is a reminder to all of us that God has always used simple, little towns to do great things! Even towns like yours!

"He decided to go to Galilee, and he found Philip. And Jesus said to him, "Follow me." Now Philip was from Bethsaida, the town of Andrew and Peter. Philip found Nathanael and told him, "We have found the One about Whom Moses wrote about in the law, and also the prophets, Jesus son of Joseph, from Nazareth." But Nathanael said to him, "Can anything good come from Nazareth?" Philip said "Come and See."

Gospel of St. John 1:43-46

"MESSAGES FROM ASSISI" - DISCUSSION GUIDELINE QUESTIONS

Chapter #24–The Joy of St. Francis of Assisi-Part II

A. How can you still have joy even when you are carrying a cross? What have the messages from Assisi taught us about real joy?

B. Where do you look for peace in your life? What have been the biggest helps to you in finding it? What are the biggest challenges to you in keeping peace?

C. How can the Mass and the Eucharist help us to re-discover peace and joy in our lives and in our world?

D. The most surprising thing that I learned about St. Francis of Assisi in this series was...what?

E. The thing that I want to remember the most from the Messages from Assisi is... what? Why did you say that?

Printed in the United States
By Bookmasters